Empty Nest
one mother's journey

Anne Meckstroth Menter
Illustrated by Taz Phillips

2-27-07

Susan,
 Since you have now entered Empty Nest, Mary thought you might relate to this book. I hope you enjoy!
 Sincerely, Anne M Menter

Copyright © 2006 by Anne Meckstroth Menter. 31350-MENT
Library of Congress Control Number: 2006901838
ISBN 10: Softcover   1-4257-1083-2
ISBN 13: Softcover   978-1-4257-1083-5

All rights reserved. No part of this book may be reproduced or transmitted
in any form or by any means, electronic or mechanical, including photocopying,
recording, or by any information storage and retrieval system, without permission
in writing from the copyright owner.

This book was printed in the United States of America.

Illustrations by Tarryn (Taz) Phillips, Perth, Australia
Graphic Design by Gilmore Graphics, Fayetteville, NY

To order additional copies of this book, contact:
Xlibris Corporation
1-888-795-4274
www.Xlibris.com
Orders@Xlibris.com

In memory of my mother
Margaret Louise Rudicel Meckstroth
Thank you for your encouragement, your wonderful smiles and sense of humor,
the unconditional love you gave to all of us. We are the keepers of the memories.

*"Perhaps wisdom is simply a matter of waiting,
and healing and a question of time, and anything
good you've ever been given is yours forever."
"Kitchen Table Wisdom"
by Rachel Naomi Remen*

**Dedicated to my kids, Adam and Lora,
and to my husband, Jerry**

Special Thanks

To Taz Phillips, for her marvelous paintings that bring to life the emotions of this book. *Taz is a wonderful young artist from Dardanup, Australia. Currently, she is pursuing her PhD in anthropology at the University of Western Australia in Perth.*

To Louanne Gilmore Pontecorvo, for beautifully tying together all the elements of art and word into a cohesive layout. *Louanne owns Gilmore Graphics in Fayetteville, NY. We have worked together for over 15 years on many business-related projects.*

To family and friends for reading the book draft and providing valuable suggestions. *Adam, Lora, and Jerry; my father, Don Meckstroth; my brother and sister-in-law, David and Donna Meckstroth; and friends, Kay Dimon, Judy Melnicoff, Gail Woods.*

"...there is no holding of a relationship to a single form. This is not tragedy, but part of the ever-recurrent miracle of life and growth. All living relationships are in the process of change, of expansion, and must perpetually be building themselves new forms."

"Gift of the Sea" *by Anne Morrow Lindberg*

"The secret of life lies within all of us in your heart...There is no station – no place to arrive once and for all. True joy of life is the trip. The station is only a dream. It constantly outdistances us. Relish the moment. Regret and fear rob us of the day."

"Jonathan Livingston Seagull" *by Richard Bach*

Contents

Introduction / Notes — 6
Beginning of the Story — 7
A mother's thoughts from the canyon — 8

APPROACHING THE CLIFF — 10
Before empty nest is high school — 12
Who's the Chef? — 14
Twas the night before college — 16

EMPTY NEST HITS — 18
Can I walk through the playground now? — 20
Crazy Dreams — 22
Approaches — 22
What? Why? When? Where? Who? — 24
List of Emotions — 25

DEPRESSION — 26
Day's Daze — 28
Release — 28
This house — 30

EMPTY NEST GROWS — 32
Neat Key — 34
Olympic Moments — 36
Song — 38
Get back to the first — 40
Where's the piss and vinegar? — 41
Le Sommet des Neiges — 42
My time — 44
Our hours — 44
Change — 44
Passing Lane — 45

OK EMPTY NEST– HERE I AM — 46
Don't get stuck in the play — 48
Executive Decisions — 50
Personal clothes hanger holder — 52
Zen's Music — 54
A Special Saying — 54
Inch by Inch a Cinch — 55
Fitness Becomes You — 56
The eyes have it — 58
Beauty Today — 59
Dandelion Days — 60
Start the Day Right — 61
Loverly Shower — 61
Morning Coffee — 61
Another Poem Needs to Be Written — 62
Epilogue - Locust Walk — 64

Notes From The Artist — 66
Who You Are — 69
Bibliography — 70

Introduction

The rush of that high school senior year, college applications, visiting campuses, kids finally choosing their college – all this hubbub culminated in what would prove to be a difficult experience for me when our two children went off to college. Fortunately, each of them fell in love with their school and with the excitement of their new adventures, friendships, responsibilities and freedoms. But I had been plunged into an Empty Nest. And I began to feel empty as I tried to understand where I was heading too. I was living in the same old environment of my changed world, which significantly contrasted with the vibrancy of the new environment of my kids' changed world. Being "left behind" was a journey, as I juggled the newness of old relationships with the joys and fears of realizing the kids were living away from home, heading out on their own.

I experienced many emotions wrapped up in my early empty nest days, and some have found expression in this book. My writing goal was to publish an easy-to-read book for empty nest moms to share emotions I was feeling, and in so doing, to hopefully address emotions they might be feeling too. I want this book to be a reassurance that it is OK to feel sad now, and that with a little soul searching, we can move on and continue to grow as people with unique and valuable talents. We can learn the importance of becoming friends with our children, as well as with ourselves, respecting and valuing each other's help and opinions and love. We can learn to uncover new joy as we center around the journey and possibilities of life's changes.

This book contains poems written during my early empty nest days. It also contains some of my diary entries written during this timeframe. And because I found myself reading any words written to help parents of college students, as well as numerous self-help books, I have included some quotes of wisdom from these experts, and a bibliography for interested readers.

Please view this book as a reminder that we are not alone. Many parents go through this transition each year. I believe understanding that others share similar emotions and fears and challenges can help us move towards this next journey in our lives. During these past few years I have found my kids growing strong on their way to independence. But I have also discovered that I am growing too, and that there are wonderful experiences and opportunities waiting everywhere for me, if I just listen, open my eyes, and take the steps.

I am the lucky parent of two young adults, and I am becoming aware of how truly lucky I am.

Notes

Diary Sequencing
The sequencing of the diary entries in this book is not in chronological order. In Empty Nest, the emotions keep circling around and back and around again, so I might feel the same emotions in May that I had felt in February. Therefore, I did not make the entries a chronological movement, but related my diary to the poems as an illustration of emotional movement. I consider the first year of Empty Nest starting in August when the kids go to college, and then moving through to May when they come home for summer vacation.

Notes From The Artist (The Artist's Thoughts While Painting) See pages 66 - 68.
When I opened the packages from Australia that contained the artwork Taz had painted for this book, I was truly taken aback - not only with her vibrant visual expressions, but also with her insightful comments. She had written, for every painting, what she wanted her art to convey, interpreting the relationship between her paintings and my poetry. And realizing that her perspective is that of a college student (she is my daughter's age) makes her contribution even more meaningful. I know you will enjoy reading her comments as you go through the book.

Empty Nest
The stage in a family's cycle when the children have grown up and left home to begin their own adult lives.

Empty Nest Syndrome
The depression, loss of purpose and crisis of identity that parents, especially mothers, feel when their children leave home.

Beginning of the story

Once upon a time there was a mother who raised two wonderful children. She had spent much of her life caring for them. When both of her children went to college, she and her husband entered what everyone was telling her she was in – the Empty Nest. The mother looked at herself in the mirror and said "now what?" Then she took a good look in the mirror and said, "yikes!" Thus began her search to find herself again, and to become the kind of mother her children needed now.

For me, this journey began next to a canyon...

A mother's thoughts from the canyon

The following was written at Black Canyon of the Gunnison in Colorado.

My husband, the kids and I were on a two-week road trip, roaming around out west, absorbing the breathtaking majesty of our western states. My mother had died one year earlier and my father had remarried. My son had just finished his freshman year in college, a 15-hour drive from home. My daughter had just graduated from high school and was rushing toward her freshman year in college. And I was rushing into Empty Nest, a basket case behind a smiling face.

Back to Colorado. My husband and the kids headed off to an overlook to view the canyon rim. I have never liked heights. So, not being one for looking over the edge of cliffs, I stayed behind, sitting on a rock, and wrote the following thoughts in my little notebook. This was the true documented beginning of my journey into Empty Nest. I realized then that my journey with myself had just begun.

It has been my desire, dedication, responsibility, passion,
To be the best mom I could be –
To raise my kids to be the best they can be.
I like what I see.
I'm proud of the results.

So now, why, when it is time to let them go
Is it so difficult? – To be the best mom –

All the years of deep emotional attachment,
The motherly fears and joys for their growth, health,
  safety, happiness –
Can this simply be released and not expressed anymore?
Can this be suffocated because of an 18th birthday?
  or high school graduation?

My heart cries.
Do I just step back and quietly say, "you're on your own"?
Don't I need more time to teach them?
Share with them?
Enjoy them?
Love them?
Where is my happy heart?

We are on new terms.
I need to find strength to do this right.
No longer a mother of children, but of young adults,
Who need a mother's care, encouragement, laughter.
A mother who trusts their judgment, believes in their choices,
Believes in them.

God be with my kids.
Help me find the strength to let go.
God be with the mother they leave behind.
Help me become the mother they need now.

Diary

August

Did I do everything I should have done and could have done as a mother? No. Damn it. I'm mad at myself. But, isn't there always more we want to do and don't have time for? Or don't think about when we're busy going through? Didn't I do the best I could? The kids tell me I did OK and they have had a good childhood. My feeling of regret for all the lost opportunities is probably because I realize just how fast it has gone – and I wish for more. But I can't do more with the past. This is now. So, I ask myself, "What do I do now? How do I approach these upcoming days to start today?"

August

It is a paradox, but I just thought that not only do I need to toughen my spirit - to be independent and keep going forward, but I also need to soften my spirit - to relax as I transition into a new approach to being the mom of college kids.

"Life holds so many precious moments that if you're fortunate to recognize them for what they are, they become keepsake treasures of the mind and heart, something to keep close, so when you're down or lost you can call them up, like files on a computer, to get you through the darkness."

"Tilting at Windmills"
by Joseph Pittman

*"Look to this day
For it is life,
The very life of life"*

Sanskrit Poem

A MOTHER'S THOUGHTS FROM THE CANYON 9

The poems in this section reflect back on the emotions I had felt during the kids' last few years of high school - and on that tremendously emotional night before college.

Approaching the Cliff

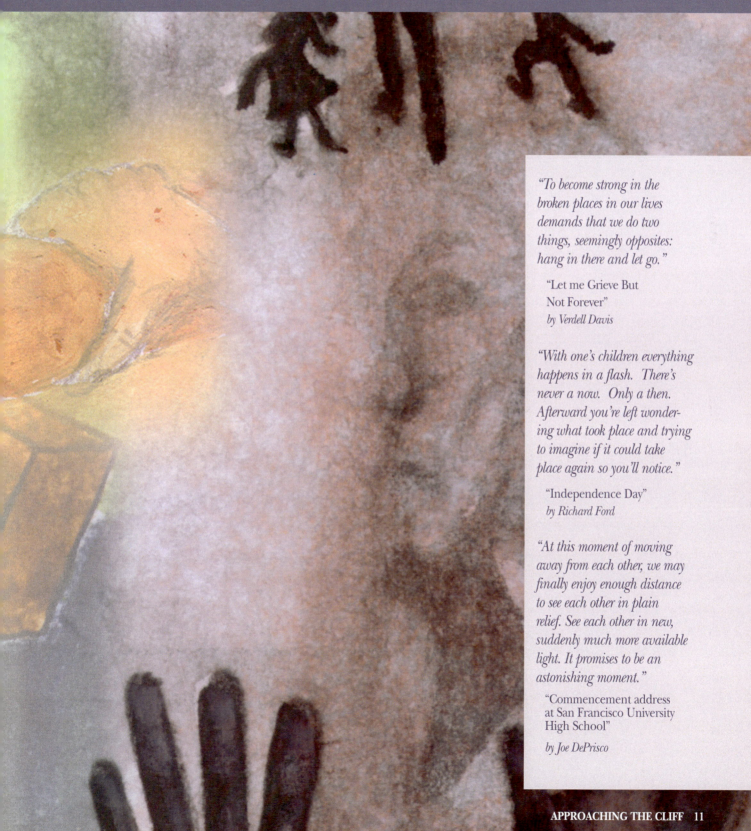

"To become strong in the broken places in our lives demands that we do two things, seemingly opposites: hang in there and let go."

"Let me Grieve But Not Forever"
by Verdell Davis

"With one's children everything happens in a flash. There's never a now. Only a then. Afterward you're left wondering what took place and trying to imagine if it could take place again so you'll notice."

"Independence Day"
by Richard Ford

"At this moment of moving away from each other, we may finally enjoy enough distance to see each other in plain relief. See each other in new, suddenly much more available light. It promises to be an astonishing moment."

"Commencement address at San Francisco University High School"
by Joe DePrisco

Diary

August

I have this crazy blend of feelings. I just listened to the song, *This Is The Time Of Our Lives*, by Billy Joel. But, the time of my life was raising my kids. So sorry, that's almost over. Where is life now heading without the kids here? I am really in a stagnant mode – not yet wanting to move forward and not being able to relax enough to enjoy the present. It is a frustrating mess in my mind.

Before empty nest is high school

I vividly remember those last few years of my kids being in high school. I wanted to do as much as I could with them but found that their focus was now on their friends, their studies, their activities, and their fun. They were living in the wonderful present, looking towards an exciting future. I found myself trying to hang on, wanting to absorb as much of them as I could while they were still home. I saw them becoming adults before my eyes – and that could make me uneasy, because sometimes I didn't know how to act around them. I was not confident in where "the mom" should be standing in all this changing.

"Letting go is a tough job but it yields great benefits. It may be the hardest thing a parent must do, especially in the stressful moments when it must be done. But when done well, it is among the most rewarding of parenting tasks."

"The 7 Secrets of Successful Parents"
by Randy Rolfe

"The mature rational part of us wants them to solve their own problems and believes they can, but another part of us wants to stay connected, be in control, feel needed, and protect them from the pain we know they will have to face."

"Letting Go"
by Karen Coburn & Madge Treeger

"I'm ready for him to go off to college. I'm just not ready for him to leave high school."

"Uncommon Sense for Parents with Teenagers" by Michael Riera

Their last few years of high school
What an exhilarating strain,
Filled with independence challenges
And mom lectures down the drain.

My kids without hesitation
Knew within our swirl-a-cane,
The tide had turned their power
And I'd turned a featherbrain.

They sensed their bold horizons
Where the world would now contain,
Decisions of their choosing that
"Effective parenting" should not restrain.

They were out and in and out with friends
Events carried them on the fast train,
While I was home sorting confused shouts
Slowly wandering Let Go Rocky Lane.

My mind struggled "Where is time heading?"
In bed asleep, yet awake I'd remain,
Listening for the backdoor to open
And their footsteps "I'm home!" to proclaim.

I believed they could handle tough choices,
It was my psyche causing me pain,
The list of things I wanted to tell them
The mom wisdom still left to engrain.

Somehow "trust them" found an opening
And helped foster the independence vein,
Days went smoother, communication awakened
Once my advice list let go of the rein.

Weeks kept falling into each other
Graduation day, silent tears hold the rain,
In their mist is a shower of sunshine,
Don't ask me it's too hard to explain.

We survived before empty nest chaos,
Faced paths together that served to unchain,
The bond of our future immerging
And the strength of the words writ by Twain.*

Home is the best space to start from,
Its passage to adulthood contains,
Masterpiece memories of living
Life's banquet from milk to champagne.

Looking back I still see my confusion
That dug deep and inside formed a frame,
Around anxious yet great times we blended
Into our unique family portrait insane.

*"*It's funny how much wiser a parent can grow just in the space of a few short years.*"
- Mark Twain

Who's the Chef?

The last year of high school and into college, sometimes it got a bit crazy with my daughter thinking I was not "with it" — a little provincial – not quite ready for the next path of her world. And it seemed to me that we were usually communicating on her terms. Of course I desperately wanted to be with her, for, after college, who knew where she would be living? So I was trying to hang on to a relationship. But she didn't need me hanging on.

While she did not often cross the "disrespectful to mom" line, my feelings could get hurt with her sassy comments or cool, distant attitude. After some soul searching, I concluded that my direction should not be to shrink away and give up on being with her. I knew that our "now" was important as our futures were calling. Telling myself, "I can do this", I became determined to hang in there, which is different from hanging on.

Amazingly, when I slowed down and listened, we could have a nice conversation. When I tried to empathize (remember how it felt when we were their age?), I could usually work my mind out of responding too quickly, or being upset and moving into a protective cocoon. A lot of this was just my gaining confidence to move forward with my own life. My daughter didn't mean to be short edged, and heaven knows I didn't mean to be not "with it". This was just growing up for both of us. In staying connected and trying to better understand each other during this time, we had to open up and take a pinch of salt along with the dessert. The following poem is written around a cooking theme, since my daughter loves being a chef.

I need to make light of your vibes, my sweet,
That you imagine you're hopelessly stuck,
With a fuddy-duddy mom you think is offbeat
And has thrown your gourmet to potluck.

My patience burns simmer when coolness I meet,
Humor serves me surprise ways to duck,
My mind's determined not to absorb your heat
Nor get bogged boiling deep in chilled muck.

We're a changing concoction, mixed with concrete,
A classic blend of fine whine and awestruck.
Can we spice thymes next course to feast bon appétit,
And unpeel life's real fruit from this yuck?

Diary

August

Hey, I'm new at this too. Bear with me. You and I have the opportunity to be great friends, but the transition is a little rough now. I want to be your friend and I am your mother. I guess we just need to step back and appreciate and communicate and not suffocate. God help me through this day.

January

I thought today about the wonderful relationship I had with mom – and remember that our close bond of friendship really came after I had graduated from college and was on my own – so that keeps me thinking positive about a good friend relationship with my kids. Stay in touch and have faith.

"Remind yourself that your child can reject everything you say without meaning to reject you. You needn't take rejection personally."
 "The 7 Secrets of Successful Parents"
 by Randy Rolfe

"Patience is the ability to idle your motor when you feel like stripping your gears."
 "Where does a mother go to resign?"
 by Barbara Johnson

"We shift gears constantly as we meet our offspring in an elusive dance of change."
 "Letting Go"
 by Karen Coburn and Madge Treeger

"Humor is the great thing, the saving thing after all. The minute it crops up, all our hardnesses yield, all our irritations and resentments flit away, and a sunny spirit takes their place."
 - Mark Twain

Diary
August

This morning:
I woke up with butterflies in my stomach and a nervous, scared feeling in my entire being. This is the day we head out to take Lora to her freshman year of college. I am excited for her and enthused about her upcoming adventures. This scared feeling is not for her. I am scared for me; about the prospect of driving home without her; the flood of memories that will come as I try and understand how it all went so fast, how I don't want this change for me right yet, how I don't know where to go.

Last Night:
I went into Lora's bedroom and gave her a big hug before she went to bed. I wanted to visit with her but she was exhausted, and amidst "getting it all together" and packing, she has been spending as much time as possible with her friends and was quite lacking in sleep. I mentioned how she had slept so many nights in her bed in this room. She quickly reminded me that she would still be spending lots of nights in this bed in this room when she was home on vacation and during the summer. With her already acquired worldly wisdom (that she could easily express at home to her mother) she said "now you can bring out a part of you that has been covered over these years as you've been raising us." WOW! She gets right to the core.

But how can I just turn around tomorrow and say "Oh, now you are going to live somewhere else and I won't be there with you and you won't be home for three months, and you really won't be home much at all in the future. Goodbye. Have fun!" Should I mask my fear with a smiley face? I told her I was happy for her, but it was a difficult change and I have not yet turned the corner on accepting that change. Another wonderful hug. I left her room with tears, for this *Twas the night before college.*

Twas the night before college...

Twas the night before college, and all through our home
The walls tick tocked the time – Empty Nest Syndrome.
My nerves were quite frazzled, busying around to survive,
In hopes that some sanity soon would arrive.

Our precious, all grown-up daughter, was sweetly snug in her bed,
While visions of 19 years motherhood danced in my head.
My husband was snoring, the van was all packed,
And I quietly wondered, unsettled at the years on my back.

When all of a sudden, crazier than the Mad Hatter,
Tears burst forth in torrents. Now what was the matter?
Away to the basement I flew like a flash,
Laid down on the sofa moaning what a mish mash.
The house was all quiet, but my mind was a blur,
This feeling "left behind" mixed with happiness for her.

When what to my wondering eyes did appear,
But my face peering back in Grandmother's mirror.
With red puffy eyes and tear stained cheeks,
I knew overcoming "letting go" was going to take weeks.

More rapid than eagles this night it had come,
And I sighed as my mind watched memories rerun.
Once a baby so cuddly, then princess toddler for a day,
Then enthusiastic schoolgirl with so much to say.
From mischievous sister, to laughing clown and teenage queen,
Her childhood sweet memories floated by so serene.

As quiet as dawn before the day comes alive,
I sensed a new inner strength now must arrive.
For my child moving on anxiously to new places,
And for me coming to grips with my new empty spaces.

And then in a twinkling I suddenly knew,
That surviving this change hinged on my attitude.
For amidst all my mother emotional strife,
I must understand this is all part of life.

I drew in my breath, saying "Don't you unravel,
Just stay calm, get excited about the next road you'll travel.
For a bundle of joys you have flung on your back,
Think of what you are getting, not what you will lack."

My thoughts now they twinkled with so much to say,
Hey, both kids in college – you have reached a new day.

Take a look at yourself now, there's so much to do,
And these days coming up will too soon be too few.
Get on with your living, your kids turned out great,
Opportunities encircling your lives, they can't wait.
Have faith in their choices, enjoy being their friend,
And laugh thankfully as your steps move around this next bend.

Hmmm, let's think about this now, you've got lots to pursue,
And I laughed when I thought of the things I could do.
A night class, a trip, write a poem, paint the house,
Volunteer, learn guitar, a relaxing evening with my spouse.

Read all those books, go hiking, appreciate nature, cook gourmet dinners,
Get friends together – we'll need each other – say, this life's a real winner.
I can move on to new places, and I'll do it with zest,
And I'll learn to love living tick tock Empty Nest.

I sprang up the stairs to my child gave the call,
And away we all flew with the van and U-Haul.
But I heard neighbors exclaim, 'ere we drove out of sight,
"The kid sure looks great, but her mom looks a fright!"

Based on the classic poem "A Visit From St. Nicholas" by Clement C. Moore

> *"One of the most emotionally laden moments for any parent – one filled with excitement and anticipation, yet a profound sense of loss – is bidding a child good-bye for college...the last big hug with an entering freshman is among a parent's most emotionally wrenching life experiences."*
>
> *"The Launching Years"
> by Laura Kastner and Jennifer Wyatt*

I began to feel a jumble of emotions with no kids at home. How does a mom react to these emotional challenges? The following poems share feelings as I reflected on being a mom and wondered what to do now.

Empty Nest Hits

"There is one moment in childhood when the door opens and lets in the future."

- Graham Greene

"Life has been massively transformed, but I look the same, so how will people know...I want sympathy - rather than congratulations - as when I was transformed with pregnancy."

"The Mother Dance"
by Harriet Lerner

"Most folks are about as happy as they make up their minds to be."

- Abraham Lincoln

Early empty nest emotions for me were very intense. I found that even after a day at work (where I could become involved with challenging projects and interesting people), or after being with friends or my husband (where I could laugh and renew my spirit), or after being busy all day with errands and activities (where I could make life a blur), I still had to face our empty house and my memories and my questions about myself - all by myself. Fortunately, the constant reading that I was doing (audio books are wonderful!) helped me tremendously. I coaxed myself to adjust to the new situation and did my best to throw a positive spin to my mood. My husband might not have felt I was projecting this positive mood. But inside of me, this first year was the beginning to redefine my relationship and intimacy with my kids, my husband, my friends, myself, and take charge of my own going forward. The soul searching did get scary at times. But I learned what I had already known - that life is beautiful, I have wonderful children, a loving husband, caring friends - and I needed to relax and laugh a lot more on my journey.

In looking back, this was an invaluable experience. I learned something very important – to keep walking through the playground.

Can I walk through the playground now?

When I go for a walk, I pass through our neighborhood streets and see parents walking behind baby strollers, and kids biking and playing basketball in their driveways and noisily running in backyards with friends *(my yard and driveway used to be where the kids played)...*

I walk to the school playground with all the swings and slides and teeter totters and laughter and little ones *(I used to be there with my little ones)...*

And then I hear the cheering and whistles from the soccer games and walk to the middle school fields where older children play baseball and soccer *(I used to be one of those parents cheering on my kids' teams, outside, whatever the weather)...*

It has been several weeks since both my children have been away at college and it is very hard for me to go on these walks. I see all the children and their parents laughing and being together. At first I tried to avoid this because it makes me remember my days as a younger mom. Even though I have wonderful, happy memories, I am nostalgic, and moments of doubt surface. *(Did I appreciate it all enough?)*

I smile at the children and wave to the parents I know – although, behind my sunglasses, I can barely see to walk with all the tears in my eyes. I am lonely. Actually, I am miserable. I miss my kids and their friends. I miss being a mom with kids at home. I miss the days when we participated in these things, when they came home to dinner and homework and being my kids. I miss being part of their lives and excitement and new happenings. *(I know I must not stay stuck in the past.)*

How can those days be gone? How can they be off on their own at college? The memory flashes I have - the deep longings for days gone by too quickly - a fleeting wish for them to be little kids again. But, they are not little kids, and they are not here, and I am having trouble getting centered. *(Why can't I just enjoy this day and where I am now in life? Moving on is hard.)*

I realized on these walks that this transition into Empty Nest, in reality, is not just the letting go of children into the world. It is the coming to grips of where I am personally in my own life. Coming to grips with personal disappointments, wish I hads and why didn't I's, if only's, and finally, well, this is where I am's – and learning to understand that this is where I am, and who I am – and to be thankful for this. I must focus on the positives and take my new steps into the future too — just like my children are doing, at this very same moment – all of us – living today, stepping into our futures.

"The best way out is always through."

- Robert Frost

"Beware of false nostalgia. There are no good old days to head back to even if we could."

"The Mother Dance"
by Harriet Lerner

"Don't let yesterday take up too much of today."

- Will Rogers

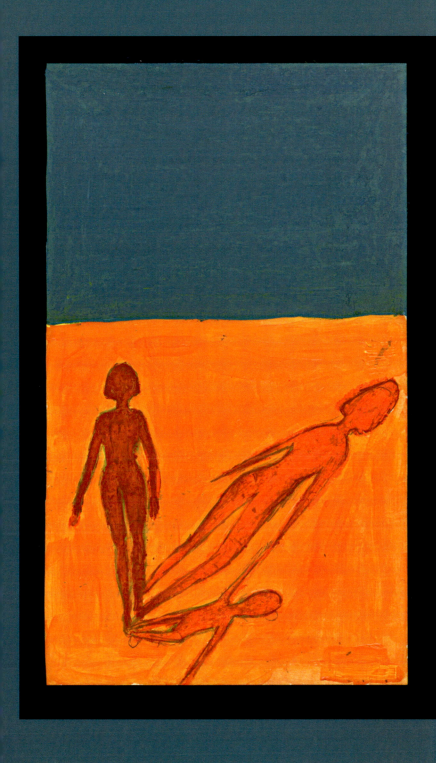

Diary

September

I have raised two marvelous children. So why am I so empty inside knowing that this, my most significant accomplishment in life, has been successful? All of a sudden I'm faced with the fact that I've spent most of my adult life in the center of my family and raising my kids. I keep crying about the passage of time. It's hard to search for the joy of the moment, for the joy of the new journey Where do I go now? Where do I begin to redefine my personal goals?

September

Where are the piles of laundry? Where are all the sneakers on the floor to trip over? The kitchen sink is clean and the refrigerator shelves are empty. Grocery shopping and making meals are different. After school snacks are no longer needed. The calendar is not filled with the kids' activities. Where are the notebooks and schoolbooks and book bags? Where are the flashing lights on the answering machine? Where are the voices? Where is the music? Where is the laughter?

September

Tonight I went into their bedrooms again and cried. It is so quiet, and the loneliness surrounds me. They have grown up and I am here in a new world.

October

I saw a friend at the post office and we were talking about Empty Nest. I said I missed the flashing lights on the answering machine and she replied, "Yes, but at least you know the message is for you!" (She has been in the empty nest business longer than I have.)

I want my children to phone me anytime. But deciding whether to phone one of them was sometimes a big decision for me, at least initially, when communication could be confusing between my mom role and my friend role. I would have a debate with myself. Should I invade their new autonomy? Will they think I am bugging them about nothing? Is this important enough to bother them at school? We finally talked openly about my feelings on this subject and now I am pretty comfortable phoning them just because. But believe me, this was a big dilemma at the beginning – whether to phone or not to phone.

I have concerns regarding my kids' safety and the "outside" dangers; what I have read in the news or experiences I had when I was younger. I want to share these with them and help them be aware. How do I reach the right balance to communicate, send my cautions and not have them turn off to what they hear as a mom lecture? I know my attitude and tone of voice are important. And I know I must have empathy, and do a better job of listening and trusting.

Crazy Dreams

Have you had crazy dreams starring your child,
made your heart beat wild,
and you cannot reconcile
until you finally call just to talk with her
and know she's OK?

Have you had to think twice dialing the phone
to break your alone,
and enter his college zone,
until you finally call just to hear his voice
and know he's OK?

OK?
OK!
This is stupid!
Isn't this stupid?
Why shouldn't I phone?
Why should I phone?
My kids are on their own!
Am I on my own?
Am I the kid?
Call the kids!
It's OK!
OK?

Approaches

Picture my daughter in her college room
Studying hard for her class the next day,
And the telephone rings giving her a
   nice break,
"Oh, hi mom!" I hear her voice say.
Then with a deep breath I start in with my spiel
And my lecture voice comes in quite clear,
"Listen to me I must say this right now,
Hear my words, it's important, my dear."

*But wait! Is this the approach that I want,
To air my concerns and my views?
With silence on her end of the telephone line,
This approach sparks a distancing fuse.*

So let's try it again, daughter still in her room
Studying hard for her class the next day,
And the telephone rings giving her a nice break,
"Oh, hi mom!" I hear her voice say.
"Hi honey! How's studying going tonight?
Something's on my mind - have time to talk?"
And this open approach can help sharing
   moods flow,
Find a two-way street easier to walk.

*"I hear you now mom!" she responds to my voice,
More receptive with my listening ear,
And it's clear that concerns sent to her in this way,
Helps us bring a mature friendship near.*

---

*"We judge ourselves by our intentions.
We judge others on what we hear."*

   - Stephen Covey

"I've learned that people will forget what you said, people will forget what you did, but people will not forget how you made them feel."

   - Maya Angelou

Diary

September

I feel distant waiting for the kids to make their scheduled Sunday night phone calls, when I may want to talk with them during the week. I email, but it seems impersonal. And I often get no feedback because they are busy (that is what they are supposed to be) and don't sense the need to answer. Our Sunday phone calls worked well with Adam his freshman year. But I don't think this system is going to work as well for me now, since Empty Nest has really hit with Lora also in college. They are both in independence mode and aren't phoning home to start the communication ball rolling. What are the boundaries I need to respect? Do these boundaries actually change from time to time and from kid to kid?

September

Strangers are coming into our relationship. Who are these new people behind new names that are moving in and out of our phone conversations like they have been part of our lives for a long time? All of a sudden, I don't know their friends.

September

I have this nagging internal conflict between letting go, letting them be on their own, and staying connected; between being dependent and being independent; between being anxious about doing what is supposed to be correct for a mom of college kids; and being anxious about losing touch and not communicating with them. How can meaningful two-way-street bonds develop in isolation? How can I prepare the road for a free flow of communication?

October

Decided to phone Lora this morning just to say hello. I asked if it was OK for me to phone occasionally and she said, "Sure mom!" I asked if other moms phone their daughters and she said, "Yes, of course." We chatted a few minutes and it was wonderful. So I'm telling myself that while it is important to have our scheduled Sunday time for them to phone home about classes and events, if I want to phone them every now and then just to say hello, well, that's OK too. I shouldn't be afraid to phone.

"Between stimulus and response there is a space. In that space lies our freedom and power to choose our response. In our response lies our growth and our happiness."

"Seven Habits of Highly Effective People" *by Stephen Covey*

What? Why? When? Where? Who?

I wonder how my kids really see me. My son asked me what I wanted to do with the next ten years of my life – and I am floundering on that myself. But, do I need to know that? He said it sometimes makes him feel guilty because he senses that I am needy, and in his mind that keeps us apart as he is trying to become himself. Goodness, am I projecting a weight of being needy? It is important for me to be friends with my children. I want to understand them better and not be afraid to talk and share in an adult/friend way. We are all growing and changing and sorting out - and I am still their mom and we are still family. The following poem started when we seemed to be bundling up emotions on our roads to independence. During this time, I have had many questions about how to approach "letting go" to strengthen our mom/kid camaraderie.

"Your greatest gift to your child is to be authentically yourself, a whole human being using your mind, body, and spirit to make the best of what life brings..."

"The 7 Secrets of Successful Parents" by Randy Rolfe

"Invite your child into your life. No one is more a parent than when knowing how to offer the invitation to transform the parent/child relationship into the kind of friendship that will deepen the bonds they already share."

"The Mother Dance" by Harriet Lerner

"We teach people how we want them to treat us."

- Wayne Dyer

What's this wise letting go anyway?
Is it for my kid or for me?
What's this "it's time now" transition
Designed to set mom/kid roles free?

Why's so much time spent on muddling,
Slow motion grasp for opportunity?
Why's the mind stuck on past patterns
Stumbling mom/kid camaraderie?

When's the safe sweet celebration
Honoring redefined identity?
When's light confetti's free falling
Plan to hit mom/kid reality?

Where's the fun spirit evolving
New connection striving forward to be?
Where's the spark found 'round the corner
Mom/kid changes discovering can see?

Who's this whole inside me unfolding,
Life's relaxed grip rhythms impatiently?
Who's playing strange chords of adjusting
To strengthen mom/kid autonomy?

What's this wise letting go I'm now living?
Why's it my song to the next jamboree?
When's the magic moment smiles welcome?
Where's the path to individuality?
Who's my kid/mom becoming?

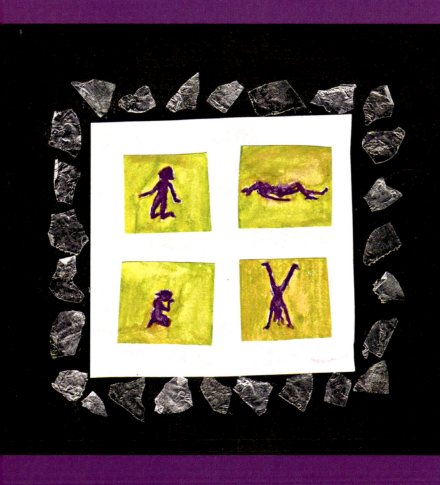

September

No one can tell me how I should or shouldn't feel about the kids leaving for college. Everyone is different. There is no one right or wrong way to feel about this. I can feel how I want to feel. I can choose my own emotions. And right now I am sad and lonely.

September

When you see that your kids are happy in college, how can you be anything but thrilled for them? It tends to lessen the sadness of their not being home. This is the way it is supposed to be – moving forward.

October

It is important for me to remember when I was younger and attempt to put myself in my child's place. Perspective affects my attitude, my emotions, my actions.

November

Lora fell at school and hurt her back. I phoned to see how she was. There were friends in her room and she was very abrupt on the phone. She doesn't want to talk with me. I am intruding. Boy, does that change my mood. Not going to let her response make me feel down tonight.

December

Am I so out of date in my kids' eyes? I need to be more creative, and more proactive in being part of our change. I want to get to know them better, as adults. I want them to get to know me better, as adults. How can they see me as a more interesting person?

December

Christmas trees and wreaths are everywhere and I am about to cry. Last year there were kids and activities to make everything alive and festive. Now it is so quiet. And I wonder if I did enough to create family traditions and memories. Goodness, this mood is fruitless and gets me nowhere. They are coming home for Christmas. Be happy. It is my attitude. But what can I do tonight to move myself out of this funk?

List of Emotions

I experienced a tremendous range of emotions as I made my way through the label of Empty Nest and into its reality. I started making a list of these emotions. When I was feeling a down emotion, I would also list the opposite, positive emotion. This process helped me think about the reality of my situation. And I found that the positive words had a way of moving into my thoughts and attitude.

Sad or happy, lonely and blue,
Crazy, joyful, I haven't a clue.
Emotions gear up,
And then they dive down
And my mind just responds
To the mood that I've found.

That I've found? What's that mean?
Means I'll make my way through.
When I'm feeling down,
I'll try a new view.
My thoughts must find "open"
To exit the frown,
And spotlight the pluses
My life's going round.

The death of my mother deepened the emotional impact of the kids leaving home and my mid-life questioning. I felt like I had been placed on a shelf while others went on with their lives.

Depression

"When our mind is wrapped around worry or fear, we lose the gift of the present moment. And it's nearly impossible to roll up our sleeves and make a clear plan when being buffeted by a storm of emotions."

"The Mother Dance"
by Harriet Lerner

"Can I sail through the changing ocean tides? Can I handle the seasons of my life?"

From the song "Landslide"
by Stevie Nicks

There was a period of time when I left the realm of plodding through it like a good letting-go mom should and depression swept over me. Don't get me wrong, I could function OK. I would go about the day on auto-pilot and was good at keeping a façade of happy fiction around my mood. But internally, I was miserable. My day could be going merrily along when, all of a sudden, triggered by an event or thought, or feeling or song, or photo or smell, or who knows what, I would become extremely sad and plunge into melancholy. This usually happened when I was alone. I did not write much during this time of soul searching for my mind was numb and filled with questions. Where did time go? Where has life taken me? Where am I heading - as an individual, a wife, a mother, a friend? Are my kids doing OK? What do I want? What am I good at? Who am I? You can add to this list – for these questions are too numerous, and anyway, are personal to each of us.

Was it necessary for me to have gone through this time? Possibly. I don't know the answer. I struggled and have come through a stronger person.

"You yourself as much as anybody in the entire universe, deserve your love and affection."
- Buddha

"In the noisy confusion of life, keep peace with your soul. Be cheerful. Strive to be happy."
"Desiderata"
by Max Ehrmann

Day's Daze

Yet, I feel like I'm in a *daze*,
  The *days* keep coming and coming unceasingly quickly without the busyness of the kids *here*.
  I *hear* my solitary inner
  voice cry,
  "This is the welcome change in life's path?"

But they say it's *right*.
  So I *write* a note saying:
"I love you. Things are different. I'm finding my way."
  While loneliness can *weigh* me down too often.

  Then the kids phone from college with simple words:
  "Hi mom! How are you?"

Encouraging me to open doors
  and find windows *there*.
  Their love helps me continue forward to
  become *one* more than mom.
And I think I've *won* my quest to belong in this *new* beginning,
  I *knew* I could,
  with time,
  find these bright *days*.
  Yet, I feel like I'm in a *daze*…

Release

Blowing deep sighs that
move faster, faster, faster
into strange noises,
not quite, but almost
screams.

Pounding the closet door slowly, slowly, slowly
  then faster,
  faster, faster,
  to the beat of almost
  screams.

Calming myself to silence
  near a sunny window today.
Sweet cat inquiring
  as the morning breeze frees the garden chime.

What is this?
Why am I doing this?
Today feeling strapped to unquestioned roles of yesterday.

Can I release thoughts to help me understand?
Can I release words to help you understand?
Can I stop the confusing pounding to begin?

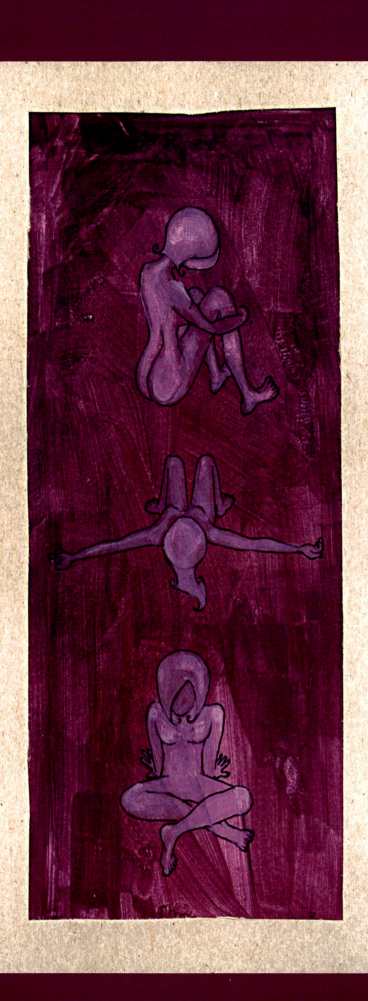

Diary

October

Many moms have experienced intense pain and suffering – personal illness, divorce, troubled children, tremendous grief with the death of loved ones – and these are all emotions that now seem to come to the forefront. For me it has been the loss of mom to cancer the month before Adam graduated from high school. My grieving for her has been so intertwined with the emotional impact of Empty Nest, that it often seems I am soul searching 24 hours a day. I am examining life, my life, and trying to learn the center inside me.

November

It is difficult coming to grips with this. I don't want to do anything. And there are so many things that need to be done. How can I get organized enough to focus? I start something in one room, walk into another room and begin something else there, and on and on. Nothing gets done. How did I do it all before? Shouldn't I be constantly busy to get my mind off the empty house and the kids? It is overwhelming. There isn't enough time to start, and there is too much time to spend. Does that make sense? Where do I begin? Maybe that is the big question, and the answer I need. Maybe I begin at the beginning, which is now, and use the inch-by-inch philosophy.

"You are the only one who can make yourself happy. The responsibility is up to you. I learned this late in life, and the power I have gained from that bit of wisdom is phenomenal."

"Relax you may only have a few minutes left"
by Loretta LaRoche

"You don't need a reason to be happy. Your desire to do so is sufficient."

- Wayne Dyer

Diary

October
We had dinner with the parents of one of Lora's new college friends while visiting campus. The mom had a great comment. She is trying to make the birdhouse fun so the kids want to come home. Great thought. Guess the first step in doing that is to make me more fun.

November
Just got off the phone with Lora. It is exciting hearing all she is doing. But right now I am home and feel lonely. While we are her home base, her life is elsewhere now, and I think I just realized that. So the college vacations and weekly phone calls that I anticipate cannot be the center of my life. It is important for me to move on. But I'm not ready yet.

November
I try and put myself in my kids' shoes, remembering how it was when I was their age. What do they feel like when they come home and are out with their folks? Hey, they are lucky because we are hip and fun loving people. I know they love us. I also know they need their space and I cannot coordinate their time when they are home. It is sooooo hard to let go of the fact that their lives don't revolve around us anymore.

December
Busy days. Adam and Lora will be home tomorrow for winter break. I can't wait to hug them! Lots to do! But decorating for the holidays has been tricky for me. I am excited one minute because I want the house to be cozy and friendly and traditional, but also have newness and change. Then the next minute I feel down because decorating seems unimportant, uninteresting and un-fun. Am I doing this only for me? Is that enough?

January
A friend who is experienced with older college kids told me not to worry about missing the kids after the holidays. "Just wait." she said. "After several vacations, you will be happy for the peace, quiet and order you have after they leave." Can this be true?

This house is so filled with memories of the kids. I want them to come home to a familiar place. But in my trying to come to grips with Empty Nest and with the change it is bringing to my life, I am surrounded with memories and attitudes and "stuff". I need newness. But doesn't newness come from within me? How can I move on while living in this house of kid/mom shadows?

This house

Thanksgiving vacation is almost over.
Tomorrow the kids go back to college.
Tonight's a rush to see friends again.
No time for home.

Why can't we just relax?
Have we forgotten how to talk with each other?
When we are away from the house, we find new words.
When we are here we get trapped into old patterns.
The parent/child roles are engrained in these walls,
In our memory house of habits.

I wanted the kids to come home to the familiar -
Sleep in their old rooms,
Construction stability,
Family roots,
Security.
But can a house keep relationships pushed back?
Is it too soon for nostalgia to bring us closer?

This is silly!
Why am I putting all this emphasis on a place?
Isn't it the people we are who move us forward?
This is a good house where I raised my kids...
But my kids are raised,
And they have left their growing-up memories here.

I need to move my memories forward.
Free myself from living today in a smothering past.
This house needs to become my memory too,
Not my tomorrow in the past.

"Three rooms empty, full of the ghosts of my very best self. Mom is my real name. It is, it is."

"Flown Away, Left Behind"
- by Anna Quindlen

"You are inherently mom-like if you have not moved on to something else."

- Adam Menter

Finally I began to start leaving behind earlier emotions of loss and to understand the importance of moving my life forward.

Empty Nest Grows

Beginning to see

"To rid yourself of old patterns, focus all your energy not on struggling with the old, but on building the new."

"Way of the Peaceful Warrior"
by Dan Milman

"Life isn't about finding yourself. Life is about creating yourself."

- George Bernard Shaw

"What's ahead is your coming of age...the discomfort you're feeling is nothing more or less than growing pains."

"It's Only Too Late If You Don't Start Now"
by Barbara Sher

Diary

November

If I bring up a sensitive topic, such as campus safety issues, Lora can get huffy and close down saying "I don't want to talk about this." Or when Adam and I disagree, we might find ourselves silently tackling a "right or wrong" mentality. Are we not supposed to express how we feel because we won't like each other's opinions? Am I sending out wrong messages, not letting them feel that their opinions are as valid as mine? I don't want silent communication between us. I want us to be friends and be able to honestly share our thoughts with each other.

January

Meaningful communication with my kids begins with me. They are on their own paths. I need to value and respect where they are, and share with them where I am on my new path. I need to keep listening better and to relax and feel more comfortable sharing my feelings and opinions. I know I'm doing a better job of lightening up my communication spirit, which has helped the sharing comfort level for all of us.

"You never really understand a person until you consider things from his point of view."

"To Kill a Mockingbird"
by Harper Lee

"The greatest gift you can give another is the purity of your attention."

- Richard Moss, MD

"Much of the vitality of a friendship lies in the honoring of differences, not simply in the enjoyment of similarities."

James L Fredericks in
"Journal of Ecumenical Studies"

"Know thyself."

- Socrates

One challenging experience for me and for my kids was learning to respect each other's opinion when our opinions don't agree. Actually, what it boiled down to was learning to listen, and, at the same time, being more open. We needed to understand that if we disagree, it does not mean we don't care about each other, we just don't have the same view on the subject. Over time we talked about this and have progressed in our communication growth. The result has seen an easier flow in sharing our thoughts, ideas and questions. We don't need to internalize guilt or feel pressure to agree, if, in our hearts and minds, we feel differently. This was a tremendous breakthrough and a key step in opening wider our mother/child link to strengthen our relationship. Relax and love each other. It makes life invigorating when different opinions spice up our lives.

Neat Key

(Learning to Walk Amongst the People I've Created)

On every subject we won't agree,
But you are you,
And I am me.
Important lesson learned,
I now can see,
Accepting our differences keeps unity.
We can share what matters,
Feel safe, talk openly,
And not need to change thoughts for the other to be.
So in empty nest life I've found a neat key,
That you are really you.
And I am really me.
And respect for each other sets us both free.

*The following poem was written during the Olympics, when glorious youth took the forefront. Over and over I kept hearing the song, sung by Whitney Houston, **One Moment in Time**.* One afternoon when I was home alone, the song came on the radio. I started singing along, and then waltzing into the kitchen. Then tears started streaming and my emotions swelled up and I began reflecting on the dreams I had as a youth, and where I was now. Here I was healthy, had raised two wonderful children and should be filled with happiness. Yet my heart, at that moment, was feeling lonely for more, and "trapped in time for not enough accomplished." I think it might be a mid-life empty nest mother thing. In reality, the self-expectations of a young woman had, over time, changed and grown. And my acceptance and satisfaction with where I am now in life, and with life's next game, is growing too.*

*"One Moment in Time" Written by Albert Hammond and John Bettis. Empire Music Ltd./Warner Bros. Music Ltd.

"It was a shabby typewriter and brought five dollars, only five dollars for what had once been an open door, a possibility, the turn of the kaleidoscope that could alter the pattern of someone's life forever. Then it was put up for sale and it was nothing but a typewriter in a pale-blue case."

  "Living Out Loud"
  by Anna Quindlen

"Our hopes and dreams keep bumping into reality"

  "Secrets About Life Every Woman Should Know"
  by Barbara DeAngelis

"It comes not from any outer achievement but from the richness of experiencing life and sharing the inner experience of life with others."

  "Kitchen Table Wisdom"
  by Rachel Naomi Remen

Olympic Moments

I sing along with the song *One Moment in Time*,
My heart sighs remembering youth-filled dreams,
Once only a heartbeat away my words cry
Are now buried deep under the seams
Of my life.

Choking tears in my passionate sing along
Lead me to the kitchen in a slow dance,
Reflecting my glory has been simple, yet sweet,
And shining moments were more than just chance
In my life.

How are my kids in their twenties now?
Why yesterday I grew up for me,
When seizing life's moments and making them shine
Were the glories of what I would be
In my life.

Is there a trophy my life can display?
On what platform can I myself stand?
That says I'm important and part of these games,
And teammates still welcome my hand
In their lives.

I have medals of honor in college right now,
Blue ribbons that shine in the eyes
Of family and friends who brighten the track,
As I search victory paths towards the sky
In my life.

The spirit of life's game must rally my heart,
And my mind needs to follow that lead,
Practice makes champions private victories show,
How triumphant a mother can be
In her life.

Moments in time challenge me everyday,
The next game's just begun destiny,
Strength o'er the hurdles qualifies my best score,
And the training? That's all up to me
For my life.

Diary

January

This thinking about what I "might have done" with dreams from my past years is getting me nowhere. Life is what it is today and I need to remember that and be thankful. I am here where I am, immersed in Empty Nest, beginning to see, and writing poetry and this diary. If I had chosen a different path, well, no "ifs" now. My journey has brought me here, to what I can do now, and to what I can do with today.

February

Great weekend! Jerry and I visited Adam at college. It is so important to visit campus – for all of us. He looks fantastic and was generous with his time. We watched his volleyball tournament. Amazing how the memories flooded back to me of watching his high school sports. Yet this was truly exciting, cheering for a team of new players in new surroundings. We took his friends out to dinner, went to the movies with several of his roommates, and then just hung around campus. Watching him interact in his college environment and observing how much he has grown in such a short time – well, this is one of the private victories of being a mother – and is helping me grow too.

Written on my 15 hour solo drive home after visiting our son, Adam, a student at Vanderbilt University in Nashville, TN.

Song

I don't know what I'm seein'
I'm confused and feel alone,
Even though I'm in the middle
Of my family and my home.
My heart has gone out searchin'
Has to find a place to stay,
The new life I'll be livin'
Has become my world today.
   My kids are grown,
   They're leavin' home,
   To start their lives now on their own,
   May God help me,
   To find that key,
   And open life's new memory.

I don't know why I'm cryin'
This is what life's 'sposed to be,
Raise a family filled with lovin'
Keep them safe, then set them free.
Look at me – my face is smilin'
Yet my stumblin' heart sheds tears,
This life we'll now be livin'
And this new path through the years.

My kids are grown,
They're leavin' home,
To find their lives now on their own,
May God help me,
To find that key,
And open life's new memory.

I wish I could be laughin'
At this crossroads where we've come,
All too soon our new beginnings
Am I ready? I'm too young.
Seein' my children movin' onward
Is a joy I can't describe,
But I'm feelin' silent rooms
And wonderin' who am I inside.
   My kids are grown,
   They're leavin' home,
   To build their lives now on their own,
   May God help me,
   To find that key,
   And open life's new memory.

I think I need some singin'
To wake up the light of day,
A song to help me understand
Don't want another way.
I just need time to learn to dance
This life with my new part,
God give us all the roots to grow
With family in our hearts.
   My kids are grown,
   They're leavin' home,
   To live their lives now on their own,
   May God help me,
   To turn that key,
   And open life's new sweet memory.

For now I see,
Finally,
The key is here inside of me.

"Letting go is an art and a loving act. But it is a sad side of parenting because you are letting go of someone you love. Treat letting go as a privilege, not as a rare tragedy."

"The 7 Secrets of Successful Parents"
by Randy Rolfe

"Words are the pen of the heart, but music is the pen of the soul."

- Shneur Zalman

"You are the bows from which your children as living arrows are sent forth."

"The Prophet"
by Kahil Gibran

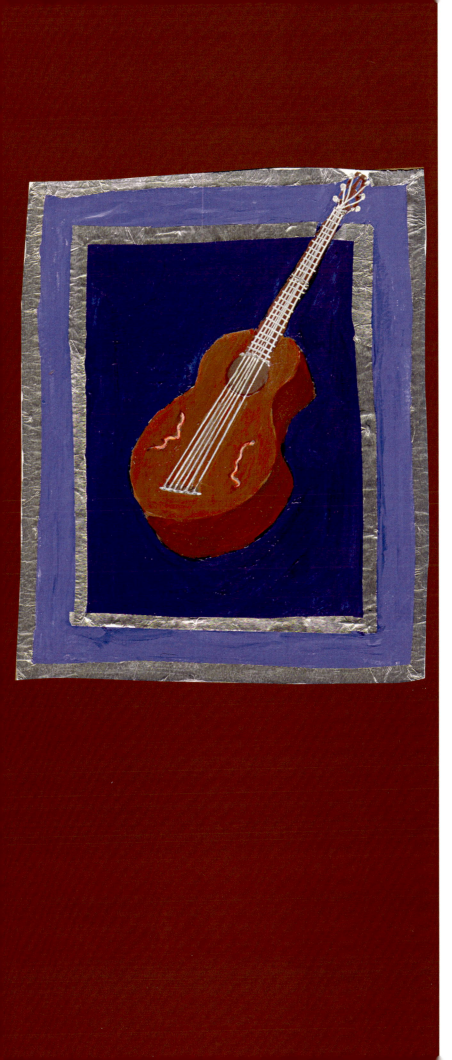

Diary

November

Watching Adam's plane waiting to take off, I think no one can love a son more than I do mine. And I pray for a safe journey and safe days until we meet again. I think about important things in life – health and family and having our children happy and fulfilled and independent. I think of other moms and dads going through this same experience. After the holidays, the planes, cars, trains and buses carry precious cargo…and tears fall.

December

I talk with other moms whose children are married and have taken on their own family role. Many won't be home for Christmas because they are going to another parent's house, or live too far away. I must treasure the time we have together now, and do all I can to build our friendship foundation.

February

When I go to the gym I wear one of the kid's college T-shirts. I am proud of their being in college and love to talk with people about what they are studying, and especially to share stories with moms of college students. We have a kid focus and enjoy talking about them. And then I think, "Wow! This time is going very quickly." It will really hit home when they are out of college and on their own, and when they get involved in their careers, and their own families. What T-shirt do I wear then? How will I fit into their lives then? Stop. I can't worry about that now. Value these days and the opportunities to be with them. Nurture this new relationship. Oh Anne, remember it is not just the kids… it is you too.

August

We visited Adam in Austin, TX, where he has a summer internship. He looks wonderful and we had a fabulous time. But on several occasions I was captured by a feeling of loneliness, since I am starting to understand that he is almost completely on his own and can choose whether he wants to take time for family and me anymore. That is a silly way to put it, because I know we will have a great relationship as we grow. I need to remember the joy and laughter while we are turning our corners to independence.

Trying to value the wishy washy "where I am in life" part of me, and sorting out the directions I want to pursue, have involved my learning to again become confident in my abilities. This has enabled me to think more positively about opportunities for personal growth and about contributing in whatever directions I choose. A restraining part of my mind had told me that my age was now an obstacle, and that my opportunities were stagnant and only available to younger women. This attitude put a stumbling block on my path and pressured me to question my new "no kids at home" worth. How ridiculous. I had glazed over life's wisdom, that each of us has unique talents, no matter what age we are, no matter where we are. It is up to me, and my effort and commitment, to revive myself toward discovering my creativity and possibilities and contributions.

"Stop spending time looking through the rear view mirror. Look forward and focus on your mission, your goals, your dreams, your future. God has put you here for a reason. You have a gift. Forward, onward, march."

- Dr Laura Schlessinger
(paraphrase from radio program)

"The greatest revolution of our generation is the discovery that human beings, by changing the inner attitudes of their minds, can change the outer aspects of their lives."

- William James

"If a window of opportunity appears, don't pull down the shade."

"The Pursuit of Wow"
by Tom Peters

"If you can walk, you can dance. If you can talk, you can sing."

- Zimbabwe Proverb

Get back to the first

Why am I so wishy washy,
Learning about me and
My opportunities
Of where I am and
Where I'm going?

First second I'm happy,
Learning to revive and
Clear my self-drive
To where I am and
Where I'm going.

Next second,
wishy washy.

Sometimes,
When I see younger women
I long during that next second
To "go back" for their new opportunities.
Vapor opportunities for me?
Why do I feel this?
Why?
How do I define my own new dimensions?

I wonder,
For my generation
Has it been harder to handle this time?
We grew up on the front end of opportunity for women.
Not always understanding our directions
We have blended our lives
To be women of time's expectations.
Am I just confused with meeting my new time's expectations?
Can I skip a step?
Can I move past the next second to the first?

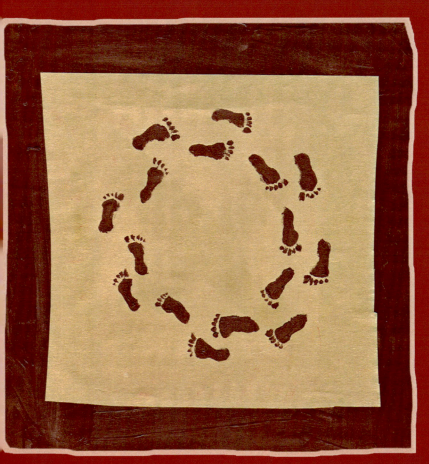

Where's the piss and vinegar?

I was going cuckoo missing the kids and spun out from lack of motivation. Then something called slap-happy hit me one morning and I said to myself "Be more spontaneous. Get going." What was holding me back from getting myself moving forward? I was doing a pretty good job of letting go of the leash regarding the kids. Now I needed to do a better job of letting go of the leash on myself.

Let me think about this,
Cuckoos tell me it's bliss
Silent Empty Nest starting my day,
Like a cat I could hiss
Startled by what I miss,
Yet the squirrels tell me nuts is OK.
And my dog's slobbering kiss,
His tail wagging with piss (and vinegar)
Says to blend a light heart with the gray,
Helps me laugh o'er the abyss,
Unwinding leash relinquish,
Joining life's craziness on my way.

Diary

January
I want to go back to college. What a life! I want new adventures too!

February
A friend of mine just got a phone call from her freshman daughter. The conversation went something like "I feel so guilty mom, that I am here at college having fun and you are stuck at home." Shouldn't that inspire moms to get out of the house for some fun and growing too?

March
I need to focus and grow myself – for myself, as well as for my family. While it is not hard to find things to do, it is hard to find me in the process of doing them. Even though I have worked outside of the home, I have defined myself in my children. I need to catch up on things I let slip because of time's obligations. What directions do I want to take with my life? How can I become?

March
"The busyness of life keeps us from understanding life." Don't know where I heard this, but as I try to keep myself busy, keep myself going, keep myself upbeat – it is an interesting thought. Maybe it's time to relax and take a breath. Maybe it's time to stop trying so hard to stay busy. Maybe it's time to stop trying so hard to understand where I am and start enjoying the road I'm on.

April
I enjoy watching people – especially women (moms) on college campuses. We need to lighten up, loosen up, forget the pretenses and have fun. We can be so solemn and serious and concerned about how we look and about doing the "right" thing. Let's enjoy the moments and being with our kids... and let's be a little crazy!

Diary

January
I feel weird coming into the house. It is an emotional mix of thinking the kids will be home in a few minutes and then realizing they are away - and I am trying to adjust.

February
Damn! Here I am continually doing things for the kids like sending them a goodie box, and not thinking about spending time on doing something for myself. I am still consumed with being mom. Also, it is freezing cold outside so my enthusiasm to get out of the house is zapped. Weather does have an affect on the mood.

March
I miss attending the high school concerts and sports activities. Jerry and I have gone to several events since the kids have been away at college, but it is different not being officially part of the school. I want to start focusing on what we all have together now, not on what I am missing that is no longer available in the same intimate way.

March
Adam told me it's not that he thinks of me as a mom, it's that I continue to think of myself as a mom.

June
Last night Jerry and I went to a music festival to hear a jazz concert by a lake, under the stars. What a grand experience to relax and be mellow and redirect my focus. I remind myself to enjoy and flow from the moment, to be positive and patient and go forward.

The following poem was written after a particularly grueling early morning for me skiing in bitter cold, wind-swirling snow conditions down Mont Tremblant in Canada. I am a novice skier and have been trying the last several winters to get into a comfortable partnership with my skis. On this morning I was incredibly cold, having a miserable time slipping all over the ice, and feeling so incompetent that all I wanted to do at that moment was get down the hill. But I caught myself, stopped and almost laughed as I realized that this agony paralleled what I was experiencing during these empty nest transition days. Having successfully gone through the rough beginnings, learning to adjust, starting to move on, and then, all of a sudden something comes along to hit my emotions, and I sense myself slipping backward to what I have already been through. I reached the bottom of the hill, shed my skis and watched my husband, with a smile, head to the gondola to go back up to the top by himself. I found a comfy chair by the fireplace in the lobby library of our hotel, Le Sommet des Neiges (Snow Summit), and wrote this poem.

"Forget about trying to hold yourself up to perfection and all the allegedly perfect people because – trust me – they ain't. You think everyone is getting it so much righter than you. They're not."

"The Frazzled Working Woman's Practical Guide to Motherhood"
by Mary Lyon

"Change is inevitable, so stop resisting and go with life's flow."

- Barbara DeAngelis

"There are mountains in our way, But we climb a step everyday..."

From the song "Up Where We Belong" words by Will Jennings, Music by Buffy Sainte-Marie and Jack Nitzsche

Le Sommet des Neiges

I'm struggling down a hard slope,
   Shivering for strength.
    Are my eyes tearing from the icy way I'm traveling,
Or from realization that I'm reverting back to beginner days when this was all new?
I must be cautious.
The steep turns so quickly my aching legs grow tense to carry me.
But here are others confidently passing me on both sides.
Why do I need to keep looking down?
Be so intent to watch a drifted ridge invisibly blend with the trail's edge?
I've been on this cold circle path before.
Let me stop – right here, right now, on my frozen hill.
Absorb the beauty of this hazy day swirl ceiling me in,
Appreciate the colors of this vibrant world zooming past me,
Breathe the laughter of this thrilling path numbing my feet to painful progress.
Let me focus -
Look beyond the powerful blast of arctic air,
Catch my trembling balance to attempt a fresh trail still.
I want to experience the freedom of gliding on my edges,
Feel the warm secret of relaxed control moving me forward down this icy climb.

Why is it difficult to start doing things for me? Moms are so programmed into all this giving of ourselves. OK, granted, much of this giving is important and I want to do it. But I need to better understand how to move through this frustration of filling days with busy "this and that" and superfluous "should-do's" that are taking me away from re-discovering myself and recapturing confidence in my talents. Can I learn that I don't have to be busy to be accomplishing and making progress? Can I stop dilly-dallying and start thinking about new aspirations for my life? Each of our lives is important and every day is a gift. My kids are depending on me to find my "daring" and move on. I need to take the initiative to channel my own growing and let my time be mine.

My time

You know,
It's reached a point when I just can't keep this up.
My mind is confused.
Damn this mother thing still tugs at me.
I want to keep doing mother stuff.
But I think, maybe -
Actually, it might be a waste of my time now,
And time I realize is so precious.
I can spend hours just futzin' around and then where am I?
At the same point,
Wanting to do so much and having done hardly anything.
What have I discovered today?
What have I accomplished today?
What have I contributed today?
I need to walk through this newly opened door
And let my time be mine.

I may encounter emotional setback, sickness, disappointment, the need to change direction, to alter my time line when circumstances don't work out as I would like. But goodness, I need to view this transition as a treasure. My life is moving forward with my family moving forward and it can be wonderful. Let me make the most of my unseen minutes and colorful hours.

Our hours

Someone compared just recently
Famous folk to you and me,
How we all inherit life's equal treasure - free,
And attitude sews the priceless tapestry.
Covered consciousness shielding my eyes,
What are my dull and warped reasons for cries?
Unseen minutes weave life, as lost patterns breathe sighs,
24 precious hours are dyed threads of all lives.

During the early months without the kids home, I kept myself constantly on the go. This was one way for me to escape thinking about the scary change. But finally I needed to move out of the just-keep-busy mode and address the reality of the situation. I am more than just a mom adrift in change.

Change

I'm too old I've been told
Must get with it or fade,
Change can mold into bold
My life colors cascade.
Toss dull gray of this play
With vibrant sweet dawn,
Sunset's ray lead fear's way,
Mixed up butterflies spawn.

How much have I smothered myself to walk harmoniously in my family life? I want to recreate an independent feeling of worth and meaning, to think positively and creatively about myself. But why has this process become so step-by-step, when I want to jump over and just be there?

Passing Lane

One mile to highways crossing,
From two lanes now to four,
The dashed lines grant my journey,
My once stalled trip,
My once tight grip
Opening to explore.

Diary

February
Riding on the ski lift today I thought about how nice it would be to get better at skiing – not to be a great skier, but a decent skier so that I can feel comfortable getting out on the slopes with my husband and friends. Then it dawned on me that it has been a long time since I, for myself, have tried to perfect my skills, have tried to challenge myself and my abilities and my mind to delve into something new, to learn just for me. Maybe this is a realization that I need to turn a corner.

March
How do I start to explore these opportunities that are available for me to learn and grow? How can I make room in my time with all the day-to-day stuff that needs to get done? Does it all need to get done?

April
There is so much I want to do in this rediscovery of myself. I want to accomplish everything at once and am going crazy because I need to take precious time to get my house in order first. Will I ever have time? The time is now!

April
I look differently at elderly people now, realizing they are just like me – young inside, not knowing where time has gone. I need to let my young at heart shine through the transitions in my life.

"Happiness is different from pleasure. Happiness has something to do with struggling and enduring and accomplishing."
  "Runner's World" *by George Sheehan*

"Don't get bogged down in the thick of thin things."
  - *Stephen Covey*

"Don't say you don't have enough time. You have the same number of hours per day that were given to Helen Keller, Pasteur, Michelangelo, Mother Teresa, Leonardo da Vinci, Thomas Jefferson and Albert Einstein."
  - *J. Jackson Browne*

"You must be the change you wish to see in the world."
  - *Gandhi*

"He wondered how he had always thought that change would lead to something worse. Now he realized that a change could lead to something better! Hooray for change!"
  "Who Moved My Cheese" *by Spencer Johnson*

EMPTY NEST GROWS 45

The poems in this section illustrate the progress I have made, and continue to make, in developing my interests, and in doing as much as I can to experience, discover, learn and grow. And I've found that a very important key is relaxing to appreciate life, inside and out, every step of the way.

OK Empty Nest

Here I Am

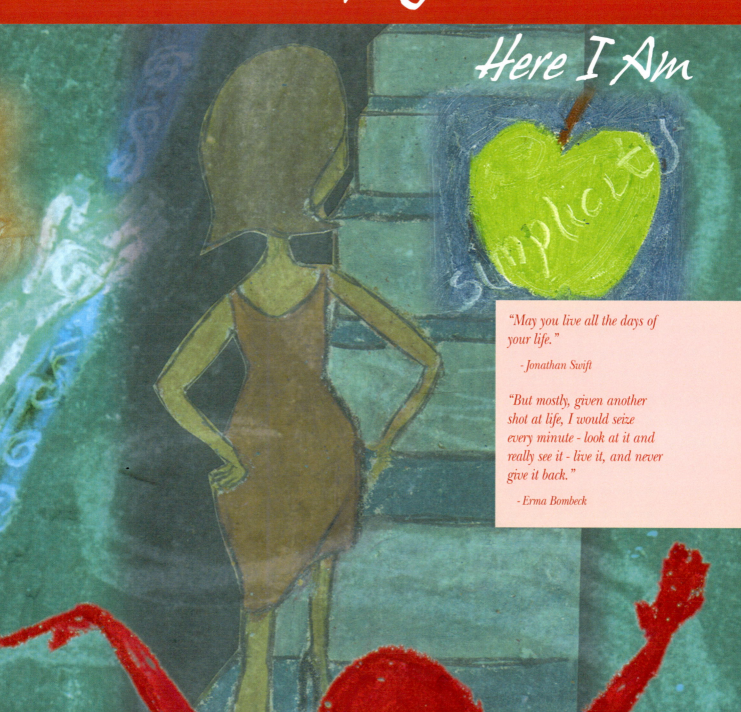

"May you live all the days of your life."
  - Jonathan Swift

"But mostly, given another shot at life, I would seize every minute - look at it and really see it - live it, and never give it back."
  - Erma Bombeck

Diary

May

This morning I was weeding the garden and had to get under the pine trees to trim out the dead branches on the bottom. Wearing a short-sleeved shirt, my arms got all scratched. I sat up and stayed there on my knees for a while, looking at my scratched arms, and at the pine trees and the dead branches that I had trimmed off. I thought, "This is an analogy of what I have been going through. In order for me to be stronger in my self-identity, and for me to grow healthy in this new relationship with my kids, I need to personally trim away the dead branches attached to yesterday's roles and welcome new season's growth." I am realizing that this is an individual thing. No one else can do my trimming. It starts with me. Maybe I have had to get scratched a little to understand.

June

Adam asked me yesterday what time it was. I answered, "It's now." That really threw him off for a second. Then he laughed and said, "cool mom." It is now, and I am trying to do better to grasp the essence of the moment... to make the most of the moment.

"I watch Beth standing at the sink and I think of my mother, my friend's mother, everybody's mother. The mother is the one who is always just there, right where you left her."

"Different Strokes"
by Jeanne Maria Laskas

"A good paradigm shift is if we can realize that the moment we're living in is the only moment there is. We can shout to the rooftops 'I'm glad to be alive!'"

"Relax You May Only Have a Few Minutes Left"
- Loretta LaRoche

I want to fling off the drape that has kept me focused on looking backwards. It's time to move on and grow; to add "me" back into my life, and into the life of my family. So why might I hesitate to try my new stepping stones? It is a tricky puzzle moving out of a dull rut onto life's highway.

Don't get stuck in the play

Wake Up! Ha! You're stuck in my dull senseless rut!
Want to glow? Nowhere to go? What will you do?
Shut up prisonous rut! Damn, I'll pull myself up.
Leave your slow captive woe and renew.

*But hey! This you say, yesterday's what shines for you,
With me stay, new sunshine ray won't find you here.
This I pray, sweet yesterday won't rob today of my renew,
Slip away, I'm not your clay or souvenir.*

*You're quite queer, harbor fear, don't pioneer and persevere,
You must cry and you must sigh, your kids have flown.*
I volunteer for all the tears, I'll get in gear, they'll disappear,
I'll not standby, I see blue-sky, my kids have grown.

*OK, this is your play, but you must weigh why you're so blue,
This new highway that you survey still brings a tear.*
I'll not portray hip hip hooray, for I must say, yes, I'm still blue,
But life's bouquet helps my mind sway towards my premiere.

Wake up! You're still stuck in my dull senseless rut,
Must go slow, I'm in tow for your debut.
Give up prisonous rut! Your damn pull has dried up,
Now I know it's time to grow, I'm overdue.

"He was letting go and trusting what lay ahead for him. He started to enjoy himself more and more. He knew when you move beyond fear you feel free."

"Who Moved My Cheese"
- *Spencer Johnson*

"You can't grow without letting go of where you were."

- *Barbara DeAngelis*

Haven't you noticed that I am changing too? I am someone who is growing too. Maybe a little slower than your pace – but it is happening. Yes, it is important to me that you see me as mom, I think – but do you only see Mom, always in the same place, the same house the same "same old"? I am trying to be more creative with my life while "keeping it all together" doing the responsible stuff required of a mom. Am I trying too hard to stay the same and move on too? Can I now flirt with the carefree? How do I truly make the decision to move forward?

"And I was struck all at once how life was out there, going through its regular courses, and I was suspended, waiting, caught in a terrible crevice between living my life, and not living it. I couldn't go on biding my time like there was no end of it."

"The Secret Life of Bees"
by Sue Monk Kidd

"I understood…the value of having a mother who had not stopped taking chances and looking at life with delight. It was comforting to know that I was not at the head of the parade, that there was an older, wiser woman moving in front of me."

- Phyllis Theroux

"Growing up doesn't have to mean growing apart. It means accepting change from authoritative role to one of reciprocity – as adults capable of making decisions and handling mistakes. Accepting this transformation means welcoming a new kind of relationship – one that is deeper, more substantive, more mature."

"When Kids Go to College"
by Barbara and Phillip Newman

"I'm getting on. Time to cultivate my own garden."

- Claude Monet

Executive Decisions

I made some executive decisions
My daughter informs me on the phone,
I'm dropping a course from my class schedule
And for Spring Break I won't be coming home.
I just got an on-campus job
And did I tell you what I'm doing next year?
I'll be studying engineering in England
And this summer I'll be…hey, mom, can you hear?

I made some executive decisions
My son informs me on the phone,
Next semester I'll be studying in Australia
And this summer I won't be coming home.
I have an internship in Texas
My friends and I'll get a place, don't yet know where.
And, oh yes, I just applied to grad school
And I'm thinking…hey, Mom, are you there?

Sit down. Take a deep breath. Think about it. This is right.
Yes, this really is the right direction.
This is where the decision-making belongs now – with my kids.
Aren't they blossoming with these opportunities and the chance
   to make decisions about their lives for themselves?
Thank heaven they are sharing these times with me.
They don't need my decisions.
They need my listening and my support.
Be there for them, as they need you now.

I've made some executive decisions
I tell myself amidst the news and my sighs,
To let my kids make those meaningful decisions
Which are now affecting their lives.
I trust in the choices they're making,
It's time to pass management down the line,
I'm the one who must be the leader
And push for the changes in time.

Yes, I'm making my executive decisions,
They involve building my own life again,
Rediscovering my interests and passions
And to my children, being their friend.
I'm jumping off the mom plank to make a dream list,
No – not a dream list – an action list for me.
While it seems hard right now, I'll get going,
I need myself again – an action list –
Set myself free.

Diary

March

I sometimes think, "if only Adam and Lora were here I would do this" or, "it would be such fun to share that with the kids." Give me a break! I need to get out there and do "this and that" because it is interesting to me and will provide personal growth and meaning in my life. Don't put life on hold. Make the most of today. Climb steps. Get going.

May

We took Adam to the airport to catch the plane to Austin for his summer internship. Another mom and dad were at the airport, seeing their college daughter off for the summer. The mom and I started talking about how excited we are for the opportunities and adventures our kids are experiencing. There is a part of us that wants to go adventuring with them, and a part of us that still wants them to be home. She said it doesn't seem to be getting better for her. Every time she says goodbye, she feels the inner pain of watching her daughter leave.

I want Adam to go to Austin to be on his own. This is the right move for him, and probably for me too. I have to learn to incorporate his independence into my own moving-forward action list, and to better manage the reality of my being the mom of an almost 21 year old.

My parents told me that the test of being a successful parent is when your children can do without you. We're on our way.

Personal clothes hanger holder

This is about clothes. My daughter is 5'11" and I am 5'3" – so, except for an occasional scarf or piece of jewelry, the only hand-me-downs in our wardrobe are from her to me. I truly enjoy going with her to look for clothes when she is home on vacation. Shopping for college clothes also brings back special memories of times I shared with my mother during my college vacations.* I now understand how important this was to my mom; and, in retrospect, to me too. Now I'm the mom, and clothes outings with my daughter are not only tremendously fun, but keep me up-to-date on the styles and on her taste in clothing. I love slipping into that younger persona when we are together on these fashion outings. And by rummaging through the clothes racks together, or by my sitting on a bench outside the fitting rooms, I have discovered that I can observe, experience and absorb amazing moments of life.

* I also shared memorable shopping trips with my father, who made sure I considered "style" in my wardrobe, not simply "what everyone is wearing." Great memories and fashionable clothes! Thanks Dad!

Here I am
Sitting on a short bench outside the fitting room
Holding 3 pairs of black slacks and an ivory sweater.
These will be tried next.
I can see my daughter's feet under the fitting room door,
Hear her sigh as the perfect red dress on the hanger
   looks terrible on,
In her opinion that is.
I don't get the opportunity to comment on this one.
Only a few items are needed before her wardrobe
   is complete.
Well, at least complete until next vacation.

Goodness! This is a bustling corner of the world.
Young people rushing back and forth, in and out,
All carrying "in styles" that caught their eye on the racks.
The upbeat background music certainly isn't an elevator tune.
Actually, the beat moves this rushing pace along very nicely.
I like it, and want to jump up and dance.
You know – I can dance – really I can,
I can skip too.
Guess that wouldn't be "in style" here,
But, it sure would be fun!

Diary

February

I received a surprise package from Lora with a Valentine and a Happy Birthday gift book, beautifully inscribed. It made me happy that she had remembered these occasions in her busy college schedule, and that her sentiments were expressions of thanks to me for being her mother. The little things of life are so meaningful.

April

Progress. Today is probably the first time that I have gone shopping and did not specifically take the time to browse for clothes for Lora. I went looking for something just for me. Now, I am trying to decide if that was fun, or if I missed a great bargain.

Oh well. Back to here I am.
I'll watch and wait for the door to open.
Yes! My hoped-for opportunity to comment has arrived.
Color's great! Fit's right!
Yet, on command I am rushing off to grab another size
  and color.
And you know what? That is perfectly OK.
For this is truly a special time for me.
I am participating in something I dearly love,
Shopping with my pizazzy 20 year old daughter,
And sitting on a bench being her friendly personal
  clothes hanger holder
Brings wonderful togetherness memories to my life,
And I hope to her closet-full of memories too.

> *"I have found the best way to give advice to your children is to find out what they want and then advise them to do it."*
> - Harry S. Truman

> *"Most of the time you can take off your problem-solver hat and put on your good-listener hat."*
>
> "For Parents Only"
> *by Julia Johnston and Mary Kay Shanley*

Diary

April

It is wonderful having our cat, Zen. Some people say that during this transition your pet can too easily become a crutch for your loss of children. But it sure helps me to have Zen share our home. She adds a calming effect, bringing joy to my days. And I can talk to her, and say anything, and she doesn't talk back or think I'm crazy – no analyzing the meaning behind my words, thank heaven! And another wonderful plus is that she helps me get exercise, for now I have more time to chase her around the house. Guess that is a little crazy! Good! I need some light-hearted crazy, joining life's craziness on my way!

"Revel in the accomplishments you achieve and in the kindnesses you receive. Celebrate the moments, hours and minutes of your existence. As you do, you'll leave behind a life filled with "oh no's" and awake to one overflowing with "ah ha's."

"Relax You May Only Have a Few Minutes Left"
by Loretta LaRoche

"Live a balanced life – learn some and think some and draw and paint and sing and dance and play and work every day some."

- Robert Fulghum

*"To see a World in a grain of sand,
And a Heaven in a wild flower;
Hold Infinity in the palm of your hand,
And eternity in an hour."*

- William Blake

"Nothing is worth more than this day."

- Goethe

There is so much I miss by quickly walking on autopilot through the day, and not taking the time to really look at what is around me. Watching our cat, Zen, one morning, helped me shake up my senses, at least for that afternoon. I imagine that she explores the rooms of her world often, and that is one reason she can immediately sense anything new that we bring in the door. She is curious and knows her world. I need to do a better job of exploring and knowing my world, even if it is my own backyard.

Zen's Music

Sitting on the sofa with a nice hot cup of tea,
Enjoying the morning paper and cool quiet time for me.
When glancing up I notice that our cat has gently found,
The top of our piano is a joy to walk around.

Her calm inquiring manner as she steps so silently
Makes me pause, for this rare moment of sweet curiosity.
She moves to eye the clock, and then she strolls without a sound,
And weaves amongst the treasures of a piano-top playground.

Everything's in order here, with nothing more to see,
She gently moves a level down to the music of the key.
Her soft slow-motion tune helps me relax to get unbound,
The comfort of her simple notes my listening eyes astound.

At last she finds the piano bench and sits approvingly,
Her world is fine, and she's content in Zen-like harmony.
The meaning of her travels brings a message quite profound,
My world is here and waiting, and with music can surround.

Lora phoned one night feeling really down, concerned that she did not have enough time for all she needed to do. She had lots on her plate with exams, papers, clubs, friends, and the first year of college coming to a close. She questioned if her freshman year had been all that stimulating. She was in a slump. So I wrote the following poem and emailed it to her. I should reread this poem, since it also applies to me.

A Special Saying

A saying I've used so many times
When a million things catch my life off guard,
I keep telling myself,
   "Inch by inch a cinch,
      Yard by yard it's hard."
Somehow that puts me back on track,
Gets priorities straight, focuses tasks at hand.
And I find, with relief, my mind takes hold,
And I learn that "yes I can".

And the following November, Lora, a sophomore at the University of Pennsylvania, needed another little boost of encouragement. Me too!

Inch by Inch a Cinch

Try not to tangle up your mind
   With all the things that need to be done.
   It can be damned confusing, a jumbled up mess
When every "to do" puts your nerves on the run.

Who has time for it all? I say the same thing,
Granted my schedule has a lot more ease.
You'll find it's a time when attitude kicks in
And you say, "I'm not going to freeze!"

All the stuff to get done, take a step at a time,
You are beautiful! You have great friends! (Like me!)
And this feeling you feel that is getting you down
You'll find will eventually flee.

A deep breath or two now might not do the trick
While you question the current state of your plight.
But it can help you to know, you're the star of the show,
Because your character's 100% just right.

Yes, it's soooo nice to get those grades,
But more so - to do the best that you can.
To learn lessons you'll need for your lifetime ahead
While juggling decisions and studies at hand.

Think of Ben Franklin*, what an amazing guy,
He's there, inspiring your campus today.
And one of his sayings is "Little strokes fell great oaks",
Like the "inch by inch" message I'm trying to say.

OK, we need to get on with the close
Of this poem, written for you by me.
Laugh a little tonight, get some sleep, say a prayer,
And remember that love surrounds thee.

Love you more than poems can say.

*Founder of The University of Pennsylvania.

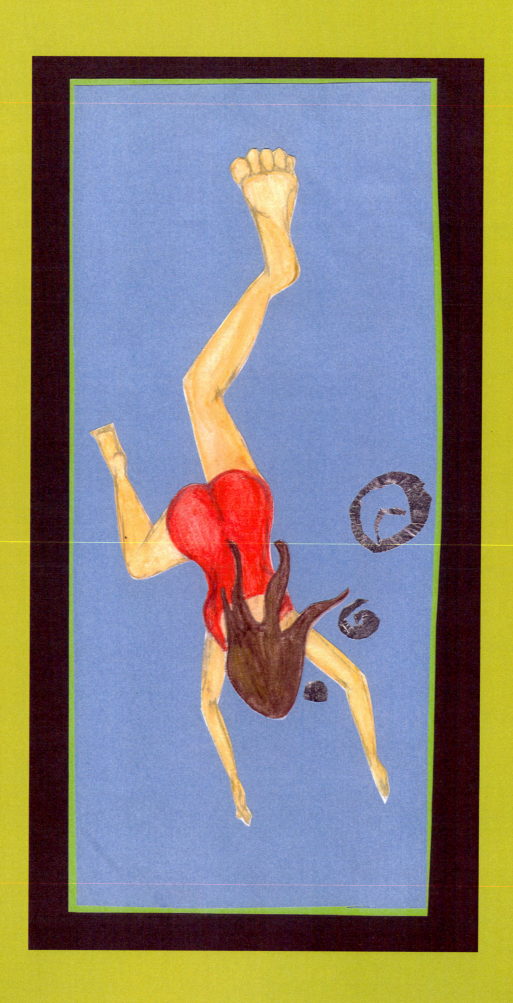

Fitness becomes you

It is hard for me to get my duff in gear and exercise – whether going to the gym, or just walking briskly around the neighborhood. I say to myself "I don't have time today" or "I am just too tired" or "it's a bother and I skipped lunch anyway". But, if only several times a week I can get myself to concentrate for an hour (OK, at least 30 minutes), I feel so much better about myself. I have found, with regular exercise, not only do I have more endurance and energy, but my mental attitude gets a tremendous boost. One afternoon I was having trouble getting myself on the road to exercise, and began writing this poem. Hope it helps you get out and "be fit". It becomes you!

I've climbed the stairs a lot today,
And errands have kept me real busy,
Can't I forget to go EXERCISE?
It's really not necessar-izzy.

My heart seems OK, my weight is not bad,
What's all this fuss 'bout aerobics?
Do my unseen insides really need a swift boost
With treadmills, weights and "walktrobics"?

Actually I've found here in empty nest days,
When I fly out, true exercise in my plan,
Muscles get sore and time's squeezed a bit,
But my mind finds release from the jam.

I feel good about myself - doing this just for me!
Staying active, healthy and pretty trim.
So what if baggy shirt and old sneakers are part
Of my fitness attire at the gym.

One big hour of time makes a difference in me,
Renewed energy, and my stamina grows.
I find that not only is my mind more alert,
But I can bend now and touch all my toes.

Yes, Yes, OK! Not another silly word,
Musn't put off finding the track to the door.
This poem's jostled me to leap towards the stretch
And run off to bounce hips on the floor.

I will run down the street and hike up the hill,
My head high, posture straight as a board.
And I'll say to myself "You look relaxed. Like your style!"
And I'll smile thinking sweat's sweet reward.

Diary

June

Thankfully I am an acceptable weight for my height. But I can't neglect the need to follow a healthy lifestyle. Keeping my stamina and endurance up, focusing on my insides with regular exercise and nutritious foods are important for my health and for my enjoying life today and in the future. And I have to stop feeling impatient that all at once I should look and feel like the fitness queen. Put one foot in front of the other and take it a day at a time. There's that "inch by inch" philosophy working in my life again.

August

I just discovered pilates and love it! What a great way way to complement the walking and weights of my usual exercise routines.

"The real secret to success is enthusiasm."
- Walter Chrysler

"A childlike TA-DAH blesses the moment you're in. It permits you to enjoy wherever you are and to realize, more often than not, that you choose to be there. If you fail to understand this reality, you are forever waiting "to be done" before you can have fun."

"Relax, you may only have a few minutes left"
by Loretta LaRoche

Diary

April

I don't feel older with Adam and Lora in college. Actually, I feel younger, because I am choosing to give more attention to myself. But my mind and my time can be torn between wanting to slow down my energy on one level (busying around doing stuff) and gearing up my energy on another level (focusing on my personal growth and health). The time is now! I choose the course. "And the training? That's all up to me, for my life!"

"Beauty isn't worth thinking about; what's important is your mind. You don't want a fifty-dollar haircut on a fifty-cent head."

- Garrison Keillor

"What you must learn is how to see life in a more light-hearted perspective. To see things with a different lens."

- Loretta LaRoche

"The face of my youth is gone forever, but so is the girl who granted that face so much importance. I like the view I carry inside, and that is exhilaration enough... regardless of how the world sees me."

"The Changing Face of Beauty"
by Dorothy Foltz Gray

How is it that some people physically age a little, especially those I haven't seen for a while, but I still look the same? Maybe because, as I observed one day, that I had not been looking closely at my face. And when I did on this particular morning, I wondered whom I was seeing.

It reminded me of an experience I had when my mother was 79 years old. She looked in the hospital mirror several days after her surgery for cancer. With a sudden realization she turned to me with tears in her eyes and said, "My goodness Anne, I'm an old woman." While she had undoubtedly felt the aches and pains from years going by, her love of life masked "old" from her view. She lived with a fun spirit and a young heart. May I have inherited her inner zest for living life young.

The eyes have it

I've been quite busy these last 20 years,
But how could I have missed the change?
My goodness, I looked in the mirror tonight
And the face peering back was all strange.
The eyes still sparkle, that's where I've always looked,
But this time I took in the whole face.
Guess the woman I think of inside me who's me
Is not whom others see occupying my space.
"Is this how I look to the world?" I said stunned,
Why didn't I notice how the years made their dent?
I've been so happy being mom to my kids
I forgot that my face paid the rent.
These years have brought me peering out to the world
Behind a face I don't think of as mine.
So I'll just have to focus on life's sparkling eyes,
My mind's face will adjust to the shine.

Staying healthy is important. But this beauty thing can be a hurdle. Why can't we buy into our "insides" for beauty? OK, it makes me feel good when I think I look good - and that makes me feel even better. And feeling even better during this time is really good! So, I might as well have fun with this beauty thing, as long as I remember where beauty lies.

"Make-up is such a weird concept, but I buy into it like every woman I know. I'll wake up in the morning and look in the mirror. "Gee, I really don't look so good. Maybe if my eyelids were blue, I'd be more attractive."
- Cathy Ladman

"Happiness is the best cosmetic."
- Karen Duffy

Beauty Today

How about a new look?
A short peppy "do",
Better color that gray
With blond goppity goo.

Extra conditioning
Those dry locks will shine,
Deep gel treatment's
Essential this time.

Move to the face now
A little bit harder, (sob)
But you can do wonders
At the cosmetics starter. ($$)

Peach under eye cream
To lift and reduce
Wrinkles and lines
That seem all too profuse.

Splash sticky facemask,
Help clear blotchy sags,
UV balanced makeup
Hide yucky mom bags.

Extra long lashes,
Brows above silver glow,
Cheeks shimmer rose/pink,
Luscious lips glossy bow.

Wrinkles can sparkle,
Face paint shout out "wow!"
We have kids in college
But our beauty is now!

Really clicking along
Brings a fun natural you,
With vitamin-enriched creams
And sweet herbal shampoo.

Oh yes, herbs and vitamins
For the inside of me,
The anti-aging importance
Of multi's A, B and C.

Broccoli and apples,
Bananas, green tea,
Fibers and soy,
Mint Girl Scout cookies. (oops)

Musn't forget exercise,
Walk and row every day,
Drink puddles of water
As you sing and you pray.

Guess it's all in God's hands,
Outside beauty toss is fate,
But it's sure worth a miracle
When mirrors claim, "You look great!"

So let's keep optimistic,
And remember just be cool,
Especially when mirrors cry back,
"Look closer! April Fool!"

I emailed the above poem to Lora on April Fools Day. I have never felt more beautiful than when I read her reply to me:

*If you wore nothing on your face
Not a bit of your beauty would be erased.
Thank you for sharing this with me
My love for you will never, ever flee!!*

Taz did not create a painting for Dandelion Days, but wrote me the following suggestion: "I really like this poem. It's a nice note to (nearly) finish on. If you were to scribble it out in your own handwriting, on just any old lined paper, and for that to be the focus, then that could also convey the same feeling...being so enamored with life, being so busy and enjoying yourself so much that you just don't have time to get everything done that you want to."

Dandelion Days

There's not enough time!
Days blow by in a puff,
Now that I'm ready
To do all the stuff
That I know I can do
And I want to learn how
And I want to absorb
The right moment is now!

But on what should I focus?
There's too much out there,
My mind is a sponge
And it's better to share this
with friends—
And I wander
And the time slips away—
So how do I handle
My 24 hours every day?

A morning shower is a great place for me to start the day; where I can relax and sing (or not sing), think (or not think).

Start the Day Right

What a sunshiny way
To start the day,
My mind blossoms like a flower.
It's time to relax,
Hum a tune,
Dream a dream,
Plant my mood in the warmth of the shower.

Loverly Shower

An early morning shower
Is about the bestus way
For my mind to kick to positive
And jump start a loverly day.
Luxuriating in warm whispy drops
Prepares me for the whirl,
To ride the rails of life today,
Squeaky clean and lucky girl!

Impressions of Empty Nest that I discovered during an early morning walk to a Philadelphia coffeehouse

Morning Coffee

Fire sirens
oblivious walkers
construction workers
bricks, birds, song.

Diary

July

There are many things I want to do and see and discover, but my focus can waiver on where and how to start doing them. My adjustment in this identity search has been smoother because I have been able to count on my husband, my kids and my friends (both old and new) along the way for moral support, encouragement and fun times. The people connection helps me relax and laugh and is so valuable during these dandelion days – and everyday.

August

Just returned from visiting Lora. She is living in a neat apartment in a quaint neighborhood near campus. We had fun getting her room decorated for this next school year. And I enjoyed taking off by myself to roam around, finding my way through the city traffic to relax at a local coffeehouse. I am happy that she has nice roommates and a great place to live this year. When she is enjoying her college home, it makes it easier for me to enjoy my world and focus more on me.

"This is a precious moment, but it is transient. It is a little parenthesis in eternity. If we share with caring, lightheartedness, and love, we will create abundance and joy for each other."

"The Seven Spiritual Laws of Success"
by Deepak Chopra

"The present day is important to you for this reason: You can waste it or you can use it, but no matter how you spend it, you've traded a day of your life for it!"

- Zig Ziglar

"When you insist on doing things that make you happy, everyone can benefit – not just you."

"How We Choose To Be Happy" *by Greg Hicks*

"And in the sweetness of friendship let there be laughter and sharing of pleasures. For in the dew of little things the heart finds its morning and is refreshed."

"The Prophet" *by Kahil Gibran*

Diary

August

Lora and Adam are ready to head back for their next year of college. I'm OK with that. It is amazing the transition I have personally made over this last year. I can still get teary eyed about the changes – but the refocus of my tears and emotions is now away from my attachment to the kids, and has moved to my growth as a person. I am more creative with my "becoming". I am finding the excitement of new awareness and discovering, the beauty of enjoying the moment and the memories, the appreciation of where I am, the comfort of who I am. As I learn to be patient with myself, I realize that life is a treasure. I love my husband and my children. I'm opening my eyes to the world, and to me, and I like the picture I see unfolding. I am an empty nest mom. How lucky can any mom be?

"Some luck lies in not getting what you thought you wanted but getting what you have, which once you have got it you may be smart enough to see is what you would have wanted had you known."

- *Garrison Keillor*

"Oh, and one more thing before you go: Have fun, laugh, and enjoy yourself. It'll be a blast."

"And One More Thing Before You Go..."
by Maria Shriver

The following poem was written after the kids had been home for a quick summer stopover before returning to college for their next exciting year. And was this me, smiling?

It's a brand new day, and we are always beginning.

Another Poem Needs to Be Written

Another poem needs to be written,
For it's all turning out OK.
My kids still remember their mother,
And friendship is strengthening our way.

The paths to our many beginnings
Each of us will encounter and choose.
The paths I select might be tangled,
Their unraveling's in my attitude.

You might say it's silly this struggle
With empty nest reality.
But the real going-through-it transition
Has brought freedom and courage to me.

I'm so upbeat right now it's disgusting.
This can't be me, empty nest bound?
But it is! Yes! I'm smiling and growing.
It's my life. I decide where I'm found.

Epilogue

My children leaving home and moving forward with their lives forced me to move inward, and then onward with my life. At the outset, I floundered inside this enforced transition, going through an unexpected depression of regret and lost time. Without the ever-present mom responsibilities that had occupied my adult life for so long, it took time for me to figure out answers to questions about my relationship with my children, my lifestyle with my husband, who I am and who I want to become. Now I am learning to live and love my new world, and I want to say, "Thank you kids for growing up and moving on!"

If you had told me at the beginning of this book that college graduation would arrive so quickly, I would not have believed you. But it has arrived, and I have become aware of the wonderful journey we all share. God bless.

Locust Walk
(Graduation Day in May)

Today.
Already.

Black robes, gold sashes, and all those swinging tassels flood by my privileged viewing.
Royal blue and red satin flow behind this stream of black,
This stream of accomplishment!

And here I watch steady rushed footsteps through my silent sitting.
Laughter, cell phones and cameras smile by my centered position,
Right here in the middle of today's pomp and circumstance.

Conversations of "when we were freshmen…seven o'clock dinner…
last night's party…mom wants me to…" bubble along this path,
where fancy new shoes are carried instead of worn.

A subway train moving below the walkway rumbles on.
There are no umbrellas today.
Tears, but no umbrellas.

The path holding forward footsteps reminds me that we did it.
And it is Spring.
And today is graduation day – already.

University of Pennsylvania

The morning after Lora's college graduation I took a walk by myself and decided to sit on a bench in the heart of campus to reflect on the past few days. The sun was shining brightly on a cluster of beautiful red impatiens in front of the bench. It made me serenely happy and seemed a reflection of where I was at that moment in time - sharing the stage with my children who are moving onward with their lives. And the sun was shining on me too - and the color red was strength and resolve - and the impatiens were my enthusiasm to keep growing and moving forward with my life.

**Sharing the stage now
The sun shines on a corner
Of red impatiens.**

Notes From The Artist...
(The Artist's Thoughts While Painting)

For each of her paintings, Taz wrote what she wanted her art to convey, interpreting the relationship between her paintings and my poetry. Her explanations provide a thoughtful complement and a meaningful perspective to the visual pieces she created.

Family Around the Table
Page 4

Anne - with this illustration I wanted to convey hope, as predictable as that sounds. I wanted to let the empty nest-ers know that once they've come to terms with the new home-and-away arrangement, there is little more fulfilling than the merriness that evolves organically when everyone reunites. Any worry about whether everyone's alright, or about uneasy dynamics seem to dissolve, and you just feel good and - most importantly - together.

My favourite bit about us kids all having left is the laughter around the dinner table when we have all returned, even if it is just for one night together. That's when I feel most proud to be a part of my family - and I'm sure when Mum and Dad feel most proud of their role in creating it - seeing us all related in this new capacity as merry friends drinking wine around a table which seems a lot smaller than it used to. It's tricky to find a spot under it to put your feet now.

To be able to advise other mothers going through what you did, not only are you thankfully over the hard bits, but it is also the final, objective summary necessary to completely move on, release yourself to the present, watch your family interact, and feel really, really good about it! The fact that you're having trouble finding the time to finish the book is such a good sign that it's all unfolding as it should, if not better, don't you think?

With all that preamble, I still found this atmosphere a difficult one to convey. I tried a few different versions and I've included the original, a black and white version, and a "sepia toned" one. Anyway, see what you reckon.

- Heaps of love, from your mate, Taz.

A mother's thoughts from the canyon
Page 9

I focused more on the context of the poem's feelings than the content of the poetry here.

The mother's posture in this painting is her way of withdrawing herself from the world for a moment of solitude. Her family is out exploring the wilderness while she finally recognizes her own needs and allows herself a time for reflection on her role in the past, the present and the future.

The stark canyon taunts her, its swallowing expanse barren for her, dangerous for her family. But it also offers her strength, with its enormous, ever-changing, yet timeless nature.

The long, thin shape of the painting implies that it is only a 'fleeting' insight into a mother's emotion. It is a thin slice of family life that can be found, and would slot into the bigger picture of many families throughout history and across many cultures. Children leave. No mother escapes feeling a little bereft.

The dark reds convey a holistic emotional state that is neither contented nor angry, hopeful nor devastated, but a tumult of regret, misunderstanding, self-reproach and, perhaps most importantly, strength and resolve.

Before empty nest is high school
Page 12

This is the darkest painting I did on multiple levels, because this section seemed to me to be the one with the least hope. The painting is a glimpse into the future, which will be a struggle to release the past.

The mother watches the circle of life from her window, frightened of the impending loss of just one stage of her own life from which she knows she must move on, but cannot. Meanwhile she ignores her own reflection staring back at her.

Who's the Chef?
Page 14

"Who's the chef?" is one of my favourites. I don't think I could really do it justice! It's just so universal, isn't it? When we kids come home after making our own way for a while, we have new ways of doing things - be it cooking dinner, pouring wine, spending time with family or just life in general...and I realize (now) that that must be hard for a mother to grapple with. She, all of a sudden, is expected to modify her relationship with her children and of course her own behaviour...

Thank you on behalf of all mothers, Anne, from all of us, for being so determined to make it work...we appreciate it in the end!

Twas the night before college
Page 17

With this picture, I wanted to follow the style of the picture-book illustrations often accompanying editions of Clement C. Moore's timeless poem.

Don't be fooled by the flippant watercolour and multi-textured appearance: Mum's crying real tears here, as she helps pack a suitcase on the eve of the rest of her daughter's life.

Can I walk through the playground now?
Page 21

She is wandering, wondering, aimlessly, childless. This painting is in the playground, but it is also at the beach and…everywhere. The horizon is any horizon, the ground is any texture. It is the World, *for that is where her children play now.* No longer needed as a mother, so who is she and where does she fit in?

Crazy Dreams/Approaches
Page 23

This image is a projection of the mother's own feelings…a bit like a dream.

She interprets her children's voices and comments as to whether or not they are wanting more conversation, more advice, more communication, or to keep more in touch.

The hands are hers, and her children's at different moments. She wants to reach out, and maintain contact, but a more self-reproachful side is telling her to let go.

List of Emotions
Page 25

I think everyone should write a list like this. Despite it's slightly animated look, however, I wanted to convey how some of these emotions might manifest…including hurt, and rebellious, and angry, and thoughtful…

Day's Daze
Page 29

(**This is a *brilliant* poem, Anne**) I think this **Depression** section is really important. It breaks a theme that filtered through at the start. Throughout the beginning of the book, I felt an emotional pattern. You begin with **This is how I'm feeling** and **I need to express it somehow,** and then it goes to a self-reproachful **But this isn't normal, is it?,** and finishes off with a thin resolution of **Oh Well, shape up, get on with it!** But the underlying deep feelings of loss are still there.

In this section, you release yourself to the diagnosis: **I'm really sad and I can't get out of it.** I reckon that's a fundamental realisation to have come to, and therefore an equally important message to send out to other empty-nesters. It's not until you embrace the sadness, and then work through it, that you will see the other side - the end of the days' daze.

This house
Page 31

This House immediately conjured this image in my head. I tried to actualise it three or four times, until I got it right. It's representative of the way a house can mean so much, but only if the dynamics of the people living within it lend themselves to calling it a home. It's something I think about each time I go back to my parents' house - which I always remember as perfectly idyllic, like childhood. (And yet in everyday reality, there are things to be done, and discussions to be had…)

So I like that this poem is saying that it's important to let go of strong symbolism if it means you are living in a nostalgic and not moving forward.

Neat Key
(Learning to Walk Amongst the People I've Created)
Page 35

Anne, I really, really like the poem **Neat Key.** It feels like a real turning point - the recognition of differences means that you cannot hold your children, revered, on a pedestal nor do you retain the influence on them you once had.…Neither leading nor following, but amongst them.

Olympic Moments
Page 37

This poem struck me as an inspirational - but a little sad and only half-felt, self-delivered pep-talk.

After I had painted what I knew was going to be the foreground, I serendipitously found the score to "The Sound of Music" lying around in our music cupboard. It seemed very fitting to have an excerpt from "Climb Every Mountain" as the background and, more specifically, 'a dream that will need…' as a motif. Because, Anne, this is one of the saddest, truest, most honest poems for me. It feels like, for the dream to happen, the mother did need strength and confidence in herself during that tricky period.

Song
Page 39

I have a tune in my head for this song, Anne. After I'd painted the guitar, I found this old gloss finish I must have bought years and years ago, and used it to distinguish the guitar from the background. You'll notice one of the acoustic grooves on the body of the guitar is the profile of the woman. The face of a sad but accepting mother who's gonna sing her blues away…

Notes From The Artist... *continued*

Get back to the first
Page 41

Wondering, wandering, stepping through. Over. Back generations of women (or maybe just me) thinking I've made it! But then why am I not riding off into the sunset to live happily ever after? We're walking around in circles (and we always will if we're seeking perfection). But if you want a real way forward, look at **Inch by Inch** and **Executive Decisions**.

Le Sommet des Neiges
Page 43

I reckon this is in essence an experience everyone has at least once in their lives. It struck me as a rather lonely, cold poem, (hence my use of weak, cold water colours). Other people flying by, and you're trying to enjoy yourself and know you should but just...can't. For many reasons you're not in the right loop, the right groove at the right time. But don't you think the good thing about having gone through that is that it makes you very compassionate towards other people going through a similar period later on?

Don't get stuck in the play
Page 49

This was the painting I enjoyed doing the most. I felt that "Don't get stuck in the play" was a very potent, powerfully determined piece of writing. In this image, the mother is breaking free from the words, the negative, spiralling thoughts that have bogged her down until now.

The vibrant frame is supposed to add a softer undertone I felt when I read it; a shade of confidence and hope...

Executive Decisions
Page 51

Strong, dark oil pastels. Taking things one step at a time. Deliberating over each decision as it comes...left foot over right.

Strong, triumphant, brave. Woman. Mother.

Personal clothes hanger holder
Page 52

I really liked the mental image this poem created in my mind, and I think it's something most women can relate to. We are made to feel inadequate in that environment - successful sales are based on feelings of inadequacy, and our subsequent need to conform and yet simultaneously shine individually...no wonder it's even worse when you're a mother...not as young as you once were...but still beautiful.

Inch by Inch a Cinch
Page 55

This poem seemed to be saying "return to simplicity," and for some reason, the apple-colour of the initial layout was very fitting... so there you have it. Remember the little uncomplicated apple, 'and this feeling you feel that is getting you down, you'll find will eventually flee'.

Fitness Becomes You
Page 56

To me, this poem, this painting, is about a new, exhilarating feeling of weightlessness.

Feeling good about yourself is such an amazing World to be opened up if you've been feeling lost, don't you think? A burden lifted from your shoulders. Swimming is a time of skin against water and nothing else. Just you, doing your personal best. A simple perfection that can remind you of what you can do.

Another Poem Needs to be Written
Page 63

This is an unashamedly happy painting, perhaps ridiculously so. I find the premise of this section (and particularly this poem) ironic, sweet and amusing.

While the mother once needed poetry as an outlet of her grief, she no longer has any time for it - it is even a hindrance to her getting on with a beautiful, beautiful, life. It's such a welcome change of heart! I, the reader, smiled too, at the happy, liberated laughter you can hear in her voice...

Who You Are
Page 69

I liked putting this one together. A little note, given to one mother by her son. It makes her feel good and it's paper-clipped with receipts and to-do lists. It means a lot...

Magneted to our refrigerator is a small piece of paper that my son gave to me when he was a child. For all of us who need to be reminded...

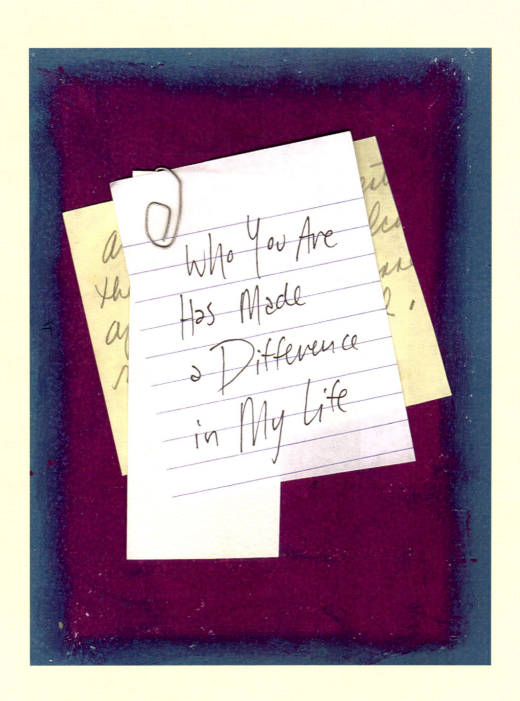

WHO YOU ARE 69

*"Read not to contradict
nor to talk and discover
nor to believe and take for granted
but to weigh and consider"*

On a library window at The University of Pennsylvania

Bibliography and Recommended Reading

During early Empty Nest I read and read …

- Parenting books, searching for chapters and paragraphs on college-aged kids, and what moms "should do" during this time
- Books focusing on personal lifestyle transition and survival of parents and children in this "moving on" phase
- Self-help/motivational books, gravitating to the role attitude plays and the positive thinking approach to living life
- Inspirational books, moving inward to the realization of life's joys
- A variety of novels and books - special interest, fiction, history, biographies

Many of the following books are filled with useful thoughts and ideas. Many of these books helped my mind sort out some of the mish mash parent stuff I still was facing and focus on who I am and the relationship I want with my children, and with myself. My book list is the tip of the iceberg in reading and only reflects what I "happened upon."

Note: Many books are available as audio books, which is the way I frequently read.

Parenting:

Ashner, Laurie and Mitch Meyerson. *When Parents Love Too Much – What Happens when Parents Won't Let Go.* New York: William Morrow & Co, Inc.,1990.

Briggs, Dorothy Cokille. *Your Child's Self Esteem.* Garden City, NY: Double & Co, Inc, 1975.

Brinley, Maryann Bucknum and Kay Willis. *Are We Having Fun Yet? The 15 Secrets of Happy Parenting.* New York: Warner Books, Inc., 1997.

Dyer, Wayne W. *What do you really want for your children?* New York: William Morrow and Co., 1985.

Ellis, Elizabeth M. *Raising a Responsible Child: How Parents Can Avoid Overindulgent Behavior and Nurture Healthy Children.* Secaucus, NJ: Carol Publishing Group, 1995.

Foster, Charles and Mira Kirshenbaum. *Parent/Teen Breakthrough – The Relationship Approach.* New York: The Penguin Group, 1991.

Gray, John. *Children are from Heaven: Positive Parenting Skills for Raising Cooperative, Confident and Compassionate Children.* New York: Harper Collins Publishers, 1999.

Johnston, Julia and Mary Kay Shanley. *For Parents Only :Tips for surviving the Journey from Homeroom to Dorm Room.* Hauppauge, NY: Barrons Educational Series, Inc. 2000.

Lerner, Harriet. *The Mother Dance.* New York: HarperCollins Publishers, 1998.

Lott, Lynn and Jane Nelson. *Positive Discipline for Teenagers: Empowering Your Teens and Yourself Through Kind and Firm Parenting.* Roseville, CA: Prima Pub., 2000.

Mednick, Fred. *Rebel without a Car: Surviving and Appreciating Your Child's Teen Years.* Minneapolis: Fairview Press, 1996.

McCune, Bunny and Deb Traunstein. *Girls to Women, Women to Girls.* Berkley, CA: Celestial Arts, 1998.

Northrup, Christiane. *Mother-Daughter Wisdom: Creating a Legacy of Physical and Emotional Health.* New York: Bantom Dell, 2005.

Rashbaum, Beth and Olga Silverstein. *The Courage to Raise Good Men.* New York: Viking, The Penguin Group, 1994.

Riera, Michael. *Uncommon Sense for Parents with Teenagers.* Berkley, CA: Celestial Arts, 1995.

Rolfe, Randy. *The 7 Secrets of Successful Parents.* Lincolnwod(Chicago), IL: Contemporary Books, 1997.

Kids in College / Empty Nest:

Arp, Claudia S. and David H. Arp and Susan L. Blumberg and Howard J. Markman and Scott M. Stanley. *Empty Nesting: Reinventing Your Marriage When the Kids Leave Home.* San Francisco, CA: Jossey-Bass A Wiley Company, 2001.

Arp, Claudia S. and David H. Arp. *The Second Half of Marriage. Facing the Eight Challenges of the Empty-Nest Years.* Grand Rapids, MI: Zondervan Publishing House, 2000.

Baer, Daniel and Greg Gottesman and Friends. *College Survival.* Australia; Lawrenceville, NJ: Thompson/Arco, 2002.

Barkin, Carol. *When Your Kid Goes To College. A Parents' Survival Guide.* New York: Avon Books, Inc.. 1999.

Coburn, Karen Levin and Madge Lawrence Treeger. *Letting Go: A Parent's Guide to Understanding the College Years.* New York: HarperCollins Publishers, Inc., 1997.

Connor, Tom and Todd Lawson. *The House to Ourselves. Reinventing Home Once the Kids are Grown.* Newtown, CT: The Taunton Press, 2004.

Farrar, Ronald and Janet Farrar Worthington. *The Ultimate College Survival Guide.* Princeton, NJ: Peterson's, 1998.

Hunt, Michael and Lucantonio Salvi. *When Your Kids Go to College.* Mahwah, NY: Paulist Press, 1994.

Johnson, Helen E and Christine Schelhas-Miller. *Don't Tell Me What to Do, Just Send Money. The Essential Parenting guide to the College Years.* New York: St Martin's Griffin, 2000

Jones, Connie. *She's Leaving Home: Letting Go As My Daughter Goes to College.* Kansas City, MO: Andrews McMeel Publishing, 2002.

Kastner, Laura S. and Jennifer Wyatt. *The Launching Years: Strategies for Parenting from Senior Year to College Life.* New York: Three Rivers Press. 2002.

Lauer, Jeanette C and Robert H. Lauer. *How to Survive and Thrive in an Empty Nest.* Oakland, CA: New Harbinger Publications, Inc., 1999.

LeVine, Mel. *Ready or Not, Here Life Comes.* New York: Simon & Schuster, 2005.

Light, Richard J. *Making The Most Of College: Students Speak Their Minds.* Cambridge, MA: Harvard University Press, 2001.

Newman, Barbara M and Philip R. Newman. *When Kids Go to College, A parent's guide to changing relationships.* Columbus, OH: Ohio State University Press, 1992.

Savage, Marjorie. *You're On Your Own (But I'm Here If You Need Me): Mentoring Your Child During The College Years.* New York: Fireside Book, 2003.

Shriver, Maria. *And One More Thing Before You Go.* New York: Gree Press, 2005.

Tyler, Suzette. *Been There. Should've Done That! 505 Tips for Making the Most of College.* Haslett, MI: Front Porch Press, 1997.

Van Steenhouse, Andrea. *Empty Nest...Full Heart: The Journey from Home to College.* Denver, CO: Simpler Life Press, 1998.

Self Help/Motivational /Humor/Inspirational

Albom, Mitch. *Tuesdays With Morrie: An Old Man, A Young Man, And Life's Greatest Lesson.* New York: Doubleday, 1997.

Brokaw, Tom. *The Greatest Generation.* New York: Random House, 1998.

Bruno, Emily. *Ironwomen Never Rust.* Nashville, TN: Westview Publishing, Inc., 2003.

Cameron, Julia. *The Artist's Way: A Spiritual Path to Higher Creativity.* New York: J.P. Tarcher/Putnam, 2002.

Canfield, Jack and Mark Victor Hanson and Jennifer Read Hawthorne and Marci Shinoff. *Chicken Soup for the Mother's Soul.* Deerfield Beach, FL: Health Communications, Inc., 1997.

Carlson, Richard. *Don't Sweat the Small Stuff...and It's All Small Stuff.* New York: Hyperion, 1997.

Chopra, Deepak. *Ageless Body, Timeless Mind: The Quantum Alternative To Growing Old.* New York: Harmony Books, 1993.

Chopra, Deepak, and David Simon. *Grow Younger. Live Longer: 10 Steps to Reverse Aging.* New York: Harmony Books, 2001.

Chopra, Deepak. *Seven Spiritual Laws of Success: A Practical Guide to the Fulfillment of Your Dreams.* San Rafael, CA: Amber-Allen Publishing: New World Library, 1994.

Coelho, Paulo (Translated by Alan R Clarke). *The Alchemist.* San Francisco: Harper San Francisco, 1998.

Cosby, Bill. *Congratulations! Now What?* New York: Hyperion, 1999.

Covey, Stephen. *Living the 7 Habits: Stories of Courage and Inspiration.* New York: Simon and Schuster, 1999.

Covey, Stephen. *The 7 Habits of Highly Effective People: powerful lessons in personal change.* New York: Free Press, 2004.

Davis, Verdell. *Let Me Grieve But Not Forever: A Journey Out of the Darkness of Loss.* Dallas: Work Publishing, 1994.

DeAngelis, Barbara. *Secrets About Life Every Woman Should Know: Ten Principles For Total Emotional and Spiritual Fulfillment.* New York: Hyperion, 1999.

Dyer, Wayne. *How to be a No Limit Person (Sound Recording).* Chicago, IL: Nightingale Conant Corporation, 1980.

Dyer, Wayne. *Manifest Your Destiny: The Nine Spiritual Principles For Getting Everything You Want.* New York: HarperCollins Publishers, 1997.

Dyer, Wayne. *Pulling Your Own Strings: Dynamic Techniques For Dealing With Other People And Living Your Life As You Choose.* New York: Harper Perennial, 1991.

Dyer, Wayne. *Wisdom of the Ages: A Modern Master Brings Eternal Truths Into Everyday Life.* New York: HarperCollins Publishers, 1998.

Gibran, Kahil. *The Prophet.* New York: Alfred A. Knopf, 1966.

Gray, John. *Men are from Mars, Women are from Venus: A Practical Guide for Improving Communication and Getting What You Want in Your Relationships.* New York: Riverhead Books, 1996.

Hay, Louise. *Change Your Thoughts. Change Your Life.* New Dimensions Foundation, 1998.

Johnson, Spencer. *Who Moved my Cheese? An Amazing Way to Deal with Change in Your Work and in Your Life.* New York: Putnam, 1998.

Katz, Lawrence C. and Manning Rubin. *Keep your Brain Alive: 83 Neurobic Exercises To Help Prevent Memory Loss And Increase Mental Fitness.* New York: Workman Publishing Company, 1999

Keith, Kent M. *The Paradoxical Commandments: Finding Personal Meaning in a Crazy World.* MaKawao Maui, HI: Inner Ocean Pub, 2001.

Kieves, Tama J. *This Time I Dance! Trusting the Journey of Creating the Work You Love.* New York: Jeremy P. Tarcher/Putnam, 2002.

LaRoche, Linda. *Life is Not a Stress Rehearsal: Bring Yesterday's Sane Wisdom into Today's Insane World.* New York: Broadway Books, 2001.

LaRoche, Loretta. *Relax –You May Only Have a Few Minutes Left: Using the Power of Humor to Overcome Stress in Your Life and Work.* New York: Villard, 1998.

Lindberg, Anne Morrow. *Gift From the Sea.* New York: Pantheon, 1955.

McGraw, Philip C. *Self Matters: Creating Your Life From The Inside Out.* New York: Simon and Schuster Source, 2001.

Millman, Dan. *Way of the Peaceful Warrior: A Book That Changes Lives.* Tiburon, CA: HJ Kramer; Novato, CA: New World Library, 2000.

Quindlen, Anna. *A Short Guide to a Happy Life.* New York: Random House, 2000.

Remen, Rachel Naomi. *Kitchen Table Wisdom: Stories That Heal.* New York: Riverhead Books, 1996.

Richman, Linda. *I'd Rather Laugh: How to be Happy Even When Life Has Other Plans for You.* New York: Warner Books, 2001.

Ruiz, Miguel. *The Four Agreements: a practical guide to personal freedom.* San Rafael, CA: Amber-Allen Publishing, 1997.

Seaward, Brian Luke. *The Art of Calm: Relaxation Through the Five Senses.* Deerfield Beach, FL: Health Communications, 1999.

Sher, Barbara. *I Could Do Anything If I Only Knew What It Was: How to Discover What You Really Want and How to Get It.* New York: Delacorte Press, 1994.

Sher, Barbara. *It's Only Too Late If You Don't Start Now: How to Create Your Second Life After Forty.* New York: Delacorte Press, 1998.

Fiction/Novels/Stories:

I read many novels during this time, often via audio books while I was walking, driving in the car, or working around the house. There are many choices to suit any reading preference. Just walk into the library or the bookstore and choose from all the selections available. It was nice to have a novel around to soften my reading regime of self-help and how to transition.

Some of the authors I particularly enjoyed reading were: Ursula Hegi, Sue Monk Kidd, Anna Quindlen, Carol Shields, Anita Shreve, Anne Rivers Siddons, Amy Tan, Anne Tyler, Rebecca Wells.